Wooden Spoon
The children's charity of rugby

RUGBYWORLD
Yearbook 2019

EDITOR
Ian Robertson

PHOTOGRAPHS
Getty Images

Published in the UK in 2018 by
Lennard Publishing, an imprint of
Lennard Associates Ltd,
Mackerye End,
Harpenden, Herts AL5 5DR
email: orders@lennardqap.co.uk

Distributed by G2 Entertainment
c/o Orca Book Services
160 Eastern Avenue, Milton Park
Abingdon, OX14 4SB

ISBN: 978-1-78281-623-2

Production editor:Donald Sommerville
Text and cover design: Paul Cooper

The publishers would like to thank Getty Images for providing most of the photographs for this book
and would also like to thank Masa Anderson, Cornish Pirates/Brian Tempest & Phil Westren, Coventry
Rugby/John Coles & Tom Branston, Fotosport UK, Fotosport Italy, C. Henry, Ike Images, Inpho
Photography, Italian Rugby Federation, Jurgen Kesler and the Uruguay Rugby Union Press Office for
additional material.

Printed and bound in Italy
by L.E.G.O. S.p.A

CONTENTS

Here at Norton Rose Fulbright we have a great sporting culture coupled with a strong sense of community. As rugby fans, we are delighted to support Wooden Spoon, and help make sure every child can enjoy sport.

We believe in opening up opportunities for every child, and we focus our charitable efforts on supporting young people in our local community in Southwark. As well as providing financial support, we also encourage our people to volunteer at our supported sports clubs, putting their skills to good use with children and young people who are disadvantaged – whether physically, mentally or socially.

We chose to work with Wooden Spoon many years ago, as a charity which shares our values so closely, and I am proud that to this day we are continuing our relationship with this excellent charity.

I wish success and happiness to everyone at Wooden Spoon over the coming year, and I would like to thank everyone involved for their ongoing commitment to disadvantaged and disabled children in the UK.

Peter Martyr
Global Chief Executive
Norton Rose Fulbright

At Artemis, we are deeply aware of our broader responsibility to society and aspire to make a positive difference to the environment and communities in which we work and live. We have been doing so since 2007, when the Artemis Charitable Foundation was founded. Each year the firm gives a proportion of its revenues to the foundation, which manages our charitable activities and our involvement in the wider world. We encourage our people to develop their expertise and professional knowledge, both through formal training and through self-development. We then encourage them to share their skills through involvement in the various charities and causes we support; such as fundraising, volunteering and visiting the charities at work.

Artemis is delighted to support Wooden Spoon again this year and the work they are doing. This is our seventh year supporting the charity and we believe the opportunities the charity provides are pivotal to transforming the lives of many disadvantaged children. The inspirational values of Wooden Spoon, namely passion, integrity and teamwork, resonate strongly.

The autumn series awaits us with the wonderful opportunity to play South Africa, Japan and New Zealand, followed by our Six Nations. What would winter be without it? So much to look forward to and the excitement is already building.

From all of us at Artemis, we would like to thank everyone at Wooden Spoon for their dedication and devotion to disadvantaged and disabled children. Thank you.

Richard Turpin
Partner
Artemis Investment Management LLP

FOREWORD

by HRH THE PRINCESS ROYAL

BUCKINGHAM PALACE

Wooden Spoon's vision is to give every child and young person, no matter what their background, access to the same opportunities. The charity is inspired and motivated by its rugby heritage and, with the tireless support of volunteers and the rugby community, it continues its vital work to transform the lives of children and young people with a disability or facing disadvantage.

As the children's rugby charity, Wooden Spoon uses the power of rugby to support a wide range of projects that are not just rugby focused; from sensory rooms, specialist playgrounds and sports activity areas to respite and medical centres and community based projects. In 2018 Wooden Spoon celebrated 35 years since its formation, during which time it has distributed in excess of £26 million to more than 700 projects, helping more than one million children and young people with disabilities or facing disadvantage across the UK and Ireland.

2019 is going to be an exciting year for Wooden Spoon as it takes on its toughest challenge yet in April 2019 when a team of intrepid volunteers will be tackling Mount Everest and attempting to break two Guinness World Records whilst raising more than £200,000 for the charity. Please join me in supporting Wooden Spoon this year and beyond, to ensure that they continue to help change the lives of disadvantaged and disabled children living in your local community.

As Patron of Wooden Spoon I wish everyone involved great success and enjoyment through your fundraising efforts. I would also like to thank you for your dedicated interest and enthusiasm. This a unique and vibrant charity that will continue to achieve a lot more with your support, changing children's lives through the power of rugby.

Anne

INSPIRING COMMUNITIES
CHANGING LIVES

The Saracens Sport Foundation aims to inspire communities and change lives through the power of sport. Through the Saracens brand, professional players and high quality staff, we engage and challenge children and young people to lead an active, healthy and rewarding lifestyle.

Saracens Sport Foundation aims to provide people of all ages with the platform for the development of essential life skills including resilience, self-confidence, ambition and discipline. Sport has the ability to make a difference in people's lives that goes well beyond the sporting field. Saracens Sport Foundation works to make this difference for the most marginalised in society within the North London and Hertfordshire community

To find out more about the work of the Saracens Sport Foundation and how you can support our work, visit **www.saracenssportfoundation.org** or call us on **02036 757 243**

Changing lives...

We fund life-changing projects across the UK and Ireland, using the power of rugby to support disadvantaged and disabled children.

Wooden Spoon is a registered charity in England and Wales (Reg No: 326691) and in Scotland (Reg No: SC039247)

Find out more at **woodenspoon.org.uk**

Wooden Spoon
The children's charity of rugby

Who we are

Wooden Spoon is a grant making charity founded in 1983. Since then we have been committed to helping improve the lives of disabled and disadvantaged children.

We are one of the largest UK funders of respite and medical treatment centres, sensory rooms, specialist playgrounds, sports activity areas, and community-based programmes and have so far granted over £26 million to these fantastic projects. Inspired and motivated by our rugby heritage and by working together with the rugby community, with the support of its top sporting heroes, we have been able to help over 1 million children and fund more than 700 projects.

Our rugby heritage gives us our core values of **passion**, **integrity**, **teamwork** and **fun**. We have over 300 committed volunteers who are raising funds in local communities up and down the country. We are extremely proud to say that the money they raise locally funds projects in their local areas.

Find out more at woodenspoon.org.uk

 Registered with FUNDRAISING REGULATOR

The story behind Wooden Spoon

A wonderful legacy emerged in 1983 after five England rugby supporters went to Dublin to watch England in the final game of the Five Nations Championship against the Irish. The game was lost 25-15 and England finished last in the table with just a single point gained from their draw against Wales.

After the match, in a Dublin bar surrounded by celebrating Ireland supporters, the five England supporters sought some consolation only for three of their Irish friends to present them with a wooden spoon, wrapped in an Irish scarf on a silver platter as a memento of England's dismal season.

Accepting the gift with good humour and grace, the England fans resolved to hold a golf match to see who would have the honour of keeping the wooden spoon.

Just a few months later the golf match was held and in the course of an entertaining day an astonishing sum of £8,450 was raised. The money was used to provide a new minibus for a local special needs school, Park School. This was to be the of first many Wooden Spoon charitable projects that has grown to over 700 in the years since. From defeat on the rugby field, and a tongue-in-cheek consolation prize, the Wooden Spoon charity was born.

Our Patron
Our Patron is HRH The Princess Royal who gives generously of her time.

Our Rugby Patrons
The IRFU, RFU, WRU, SRU, RFL all support us in our charitable work.

Sporting Partners
We work closely with a variety of clubs, league associations and governing bodies who help us achieve our vision of improving young lives though the power of rugby.

    RFL **PREMIERSHIP RUGBY**

HITZ' big impact

While focused on lifting the skills of teenagers not in education, employment or training rather than trophies, the Wooden Spoon-supported HITZ programme boasts a win rate any team would envy.

Delivered by Premiership Rugby clubs, the social inclusion scheme supports 400 young people each year by entering them into personalised study programmes or traineeships. An incredible 80% complete the course, of which 70% progress into further education, training or employment.

And the stories of the names behind the numbers are equally impressive.

Ben, for example, spent most of his school years crippled by self-doubt as a consequence of his attention deficit hyperactivity disorder (ADHD).

"Ben has found life quite hard," confided his mum, Joanne. "He used to hit out a lot, throw things and would dive down concrete stairs without even thinking. At one point I thought 'he's not going to make adulthood if he goes on like this'.

"He has struggled to believe that he is capable of doing things."

However, taking part in London Irish HITZ — which was set up in 2009 with the aim of using rugby's ethos and role models to combat the challenges facing Britain's youth — has transformed the 18-year-old's outlook on life.

"I am more confident than ever, I've really pushed hard and gained qualifications after three years of trying and I'm looking at a possible apprenticeship," said Ben. "Everything is going right and the way I feel now I just don't want to stop. My future is very bright."

woodenspoon.org.uk/membership   **#wearerugby**

Wooden Spoon Schools campaign
supported by Gullivers Sports Travel

Play your socks off for Wooden Spoon, the children's charity of rugby!

Launched in 2017, our Schools campaign supported by Gullivers Sports Travel is an exciting initiative where students can wear Wooden Spoon rugby socks for a match and help to raise vital funds for local projects. Our distinctive stripy socks cost £10 a pair, which includes a £5 donation. **Join in the fun and stand out on the rugby pitch in 2018/19.**

For more information about this great campaign please visit **woodenspoon.org.uk/schools** or call **01252 773720**

Wooden Spoon is a registered charity in England and Wales
(Reg No: 326691) and in Scotland (Reg No: SC039247)

   RFL PREMIERSHIP **RUGBY**

(FR) Registered with **FUNDRAISING REGULATOR**

woodenspoon.org.uk/membership 📷 @charityspoon

Join our club!

Become a member of Wooden Spoon for just £5 a month and help us change children's lives.

Members can:

- Win rugby tickets
- Hear from our projects
- Get a free gift
- Receive our magazine

And most importantly, you will be helping change the lives of children and young people with disabilities or facing disadvantage across the UK & Ireland.

Wooden Spoon is a registered charity in England and Wales (Reg No: 326691) and in Scotland (Reg No: SC039247)

woodenspoon.org.uk/membership   **#wearerugby**

1

MMENT
& FEATURES

Siya Kolisi
TOUCHING THE HEART OF A NATION

by MICK CLEARY

'You can't play to be the best black player or to be the best white player to appeal to a community; you have to play to be the best for every South African. We represent something much bigger than we can imagine.'

South Africans are not an easy race to win over. They have lived through hard times, challenging times, disruptive and dehumanising times. For all the challenges that each and every national rugby coach in the world faces, the degree of difficulty in their jobs comes nowhere near the task facing a Springbok coach. Those who say sport and politics should not mix have never been to South Africa where sport is politics and, given the history of the country, rightly so.

And that, in a nutshell, is why the appointment of Siya Kolisi as Springbok captain for the first Test against England at Ellis Park in June 2018 was one of the seminal moments in sport. In 1995 Nelson Mandela held the rugby world in his magnetic grip as he strode to the podium wearing the no. 6 jersey of South Africa captain Francois Pienaar as the World Cup was won, the visible incarnation of the rainbow nation. The sight of Mandela in the shirt was power-dressing at its most resonant. But it was also gesture politics, a powerful symbol in its way, signalling that it was all right for blacks to cheer for the sport of the Afrikaners, but it was only the start point.

ABOVE Siya Kolisi poses with head coach Rassie Erasmus during the media session before the first Test with England, June 2018.

LEFT Kolisi leads out his team at Ellis Park, Johannesburg, for the first Test, 9 June 2018.

Mandela had shown the way. It has taken over two decades more for there to be any real sign of proper commitment to that cause.

And there is still much more to do. But Kolisi's arrival into the position on merit rather than as a sop to political correctness or transformation edicts is a turning point. That much was in evidence in the build-up to that first Test in Johannesburg and confirmed as he ran out on to the Ellis Park field, acclaimed by the capacity crowd packed into the stadium on that day. They were saluting not just the new Springbok captain but also the man himself as well as the moment.

Quite what they were thinking some twenty minutes later as Kolisi gathered his green-shirted teammates round him under the posts to preach some words of wisdom after the Springboks had conceded their third try to England within the opening quarter is anyone's guess. But he believed, the team believed and, after one of the most startling comebacks in the history of the game, the country believed as the Springboks fought back to win the first Test, 42–39.

Whatever happens over the coming months and years, the Kolisi story will not fade. It was a seminal act in the history not only of the Springboks but also of South Africa. Much as the '95 triumph and the Mandela jig of delight on the podium provided rich Hollywood source material for *Invictus* (starring Matt Damon as Pienaar), so you might imagine that Kolisi's journey from the impoverished Port Elizabeth township of Zwide, where his favourite 'toy' was a mere brick, to leading the Springboks might also one day be turned into a film.

It is a remarkable achievement, Kolisi rising from a place where getting a scrap of food on the table was the main objective of the day. 'Times were tough when I was little and often there wasn't food,' said Kolisi. 'I would go to bed starving. Sometimes we didn't have enough money to pay my primary school fees, which were only R50 [£3] a year.'

The mighty Springboks belonged to another realm of experience.

'You don't have those dreams when you are in a township,' said Kolisi, as honest and articulate in his comments as he is in his play, only realising of such possibilities when he was spotted by a talent scout and offered a scholarship to the prestigious Grey School in Port Elizabeth. 'That was when I started dreaming

differently. From the first time I picked up a rugby ball and ran with it, I wanted to wear that green jersey. I remember my heart became so hot I wanted to burst with excitement.'

Those who were closest to him in those days recognised a depth of character that was to take him far, even if that evidence had an inauspicious start when Kolisi joined his new classmates as a 14-year-old for a routine Test where they jumped into the Grey HS pool for a 30-length exercise. Kolisi did not demur, even though he couldn't actually swim. 'Siya sank straight to the bottom but when he was pulled out he came up with a smile on his face, saying "Jeez, that's not as easy as it looks,"' the then Grey HS 1st XV coach Dean Carelse told the *Daily Telegraph*. 'Siya embraced every test, every obstacle, every experience.'

Six months later Kolisi was playing for the school water-polo team. Kolisi was one of three boys from the Zwide township who had been spotted by Greys' coach Andrew Hayidakis, and given bursaries to attend one of the most prestigious schools in the country, the *alma mater* of England's Mike Catt as well as South African cricketer Graeme Pollock.

'He was quite small when he first came to us as a 13-year-old so he had to be smart on the field, boxing clever to put others into space,' said Carelse who used to help with food and other things, toothpaste even. 'But Siya always thought of others first, in life as well as in sport.'

But he knew his own mind, too, acutely aware of who he was and where he came from. Carelse used to drop him back to Zwide after training.

'His township pals would tease him as he got out of the car, telling him that he was too good for them now, going to the big white school,' said Carelse. 'Some other boys we had had at Greys in similar situations used to change out of their rugby kit or school uniform before they got back to the township. But not Siya. He was proud of what he was doing and the opportunity he had been given. He has become a cult hero there, a beacon of hope. And he has done it by being himself.'

That singular trait has continued right through his playing career, from the unfussy, grafting figure on the field, doing the basic chores of a flanker without fear or favour, winning turnovers, hitting hard, always putting the team first, to the down-to-earth, measured character thrust into the spotlight, the focus of so much interest for the simple colour of his skin. Yet Kolisi did not waver, did not try to play to the camera or to avoid the significance of the occasion. He recognised that it was a big deal even if his prime focus was the game itself. If

Kolisi had been trained by PR experts for weeks – and he wasn't, relying instead on the shrewd, empathetic influence of the Springbok management led by head coach, Rassie Erasmus – he could not have handled it better. You can't fake sincerity.

'I hope I get to inspire not only black people but every South African because I don't only represent black people but the whole country,' said Kolisi as he prepared to lead the Springboks for the first time. 'Saturday will be the first time when everything comes together and I realise how big this moment is. Ellis Park is a really special field, to sing the national anthem and it is sent out equally from the people. You are staring at the crowd and you see the whole of South Africa in front of you, all different races, all different colours, it is really beautiful. It is one of the most beautiful things I have ever seen. It feels like this is a new beginning for all of us, that we are all in the same boat. I don't shy away from where I have come from and I'm aware that my story is a typical South African story in some ways. It's my motivation. Yes, being a professional sportsman can be tough and occasionally you question if it's all worth it. But then I just think about where I've come from and about the people that look up to me. For me to be able to help people inspired by me, I have to play every week. That is my duty. I tell my team-mates that you should never play just to represent one group. You can't play to be the best black player or to be the best white player to appeal to a community; you have to play to be the best for every South African. We represent something much bigger than we can imagine.'

South Africa agrees, from respected commentator Mark Keohane, who believes that Erasmus did more for the future of Springbok rugby in the space of a month in and around the England Test series than any of his predecessors with his enlightened and sincere commitment to having 50 per cent representation by the 2019 World Cup while also being successful on the field, to respected local journalist Simnikiwe Xabanisa, who spoke from the heart when writing after that dramatic first Test:

'I have written about rugby for 18 years and in that time I have seen some serious lows and been privileged enough to have written about a World Cup final [2007] that the Springboks won. But even that pales in significance to reporting on yesterday's game [the first Test] – at long last I feel like I belong.'

Winning hearts and minds as well as Test matches, Kolisi is quite an act.

LEFT Siya Kolisi (right), the first non-white Springbok captain, sings the national anthem with team mates Tendai Mtawarira and Bongi Mbonambi (left), Ellis Park, 9 June 2018.

BELOW Kolisi in action for the Stormers during their Super Rugby 29–17 victory over the Bulls at Newlands Stadium in May 2018.

A New Women's League
TYRRELLS PREMIER 15s

by SARA ORCHARD

'We wanted to put in place a competition that was aspirational for younger players. We hope to double the number of women and girls playing the game over the next four years to 50,000 players.'

Top-flight women's club rugby in England was revamped and given a new identity in the 2017–18 season. A new league was launched and, having attracted its own sponsor, the Tyrrells Premier 15s was born. The ten teams that competed had won franchises following a selection process by the RFU. Amongst a number of guarantees, each club had to offer its players physiotherapy and medical support, and have a stadium that had the capability to broadcast its matches live. The RFU invested £2.4m into the league over three years, with the aim of reducing the performance gap between the England XV and the club game.

At the September launch of the league the RFU's Director of Professional Rugby, Nigel Melville, explained: 'We wanted to put in place a competition that was aspirational for younger players. We hope to double the number of women and girls playing the game over the next four years to 50,000 players and a lot of them will want to participate in this league.'

Former England international Danielle Waterman knew that top-level domestic rugby for women in England had to evolve: 'Until this season, the women's club game had been reliant mainly on volunteers delivering the programmes at each club. Although many have done an excellent job, by offering these as paid positions, people

have the opportunity to focus more on the role they have, and are also accountable for performance and delivery.'

'Now not only international players have access to strength and conditioning programmes, video analysis, regular coaching outside of designated club time, physiotherapy and medical cover. It means clubs are producing better athletes within our game and that in turn is increasing the standard across the league.'

The Rugby Football Union's women's head of performance, Nicky Ponsford, has frequently spoken about how different women's sports have come together to share best practice and how rugby union has learnt from its sporting sisters. The Premier 15s was part created in response to the success seen in other revamped women's leagues, in particular the Women's Super Leagues in football and netball, along with the popularity of top-flight competitions in hockey and cricket.

The Premier 15s remains amateur but many clubs made statements with high-profile player moves across the league. Richmond captured the signing of former France captain Gaelle Mignot while new entrant to the leagues Loughborough Lightning persuaded England captain Sarah Hunter to join as a player–coach from Bristol.

Saracens Women's coach Rob Cain was impressed with both the international and domestic talent that the Premier 15s attracted: 'Harlequins signing Aldora Itunu from New Zealand's victorious World Cup-winning side along with England's Abbie Scott were significant. Then there was Gloucester–Hartpury signing England's Sarah Bern and Bianca Blackburn. Wasps signed a few England players, in particular Nolli [Danielle] Waterman and I imagine we [Saracens] took everyone by surprise by resigning Poppy Cleall and signing Marlie Packer.'

On the subject of securing Red Roses flanker Packer, Cain said he was determined to bring her to Saracens from Bristol: 'It was the right time for both her and the club. Marlie has some wonderful qualities that I have always admired and wanted to have at Saracens.' Packer was persuaded by Cain to make the shift to Saracens despite still living in the West Country and commuting to North London for games and training. Luckily she could do most of her travelling in her work van from Home Serve, for whom she still works as a plumber.

Cain explained his pursuit of Packer, a 2014 World Cup winner with England, was for more than just her experience and physicality on the rugby pitch: 'With such a young squad she was able to be a natural leader. I have been lucky enough to have worked with some of the best sevens and XVs players and she is right up there with the best of them.'

Packer would join a dominant Saracens back row alongside the Cleall sisters, identical twins Poppy and Bryony. The partnership between the three would prove significant in the success Saracens would enjoy as the season progressed.

ABOVE Beth Stott's penalty gave Waterloo Ladies a 3–0 half-time lead during the Tyrrells Premier 15 game at the Memorial Ground, on 16 September 2017, the new league's opening day. Saracens took the game 22–13 after a late comeback.

RIGHT Lottie Clapp of Saracens Women scores their second try during the Tyrrells Premier 15s Final with Harlequins Ladies at the Ealing Trailfinders ground, 29 April 2018.

Meanwhile Waterman's move from Bristol to Wasps was another high-profile switch. The 2014 World Cup winner wanted to move closer to London but the draw of Wasps coach Giselle Mather persuaded her to go to Wasps: 'Out of all the clubs in the area, the main pull was Giselle. She is an incredible coach and people-manager, and I have loved the time playing under her so far.'

The RFU would stream at least five of the matches while Sky Sports also committed to broadcasting the final. Media interest rose in comparison to the old Women's Premiership and the Harlequins joint head coach Gary Street joked at one point that he had friends who didn't even know that there had been a women's league before the Tyrrells Premier 15s was launched.

With an increase in funding and media interest, Harlequins Ladies set themselves the target of attracting a record crowd for a domestic women's club game. They selected their home fixture with local rivals Richmond in March 2018 to try and fill the stands at the Twickenham Stoop. It was difficult to stand up previous women's club records as many matches were not ticketed or were played as double-headers with men's fixtures. The Harlequins–Richmond match attracted 4,542 and has now set the benchmark for future seasons.

The league's format followed that of the men's Premiership. After 18 rounds in which the ten sides all played each other home and away once, the top four went into the semi-finals. Differences from the men's league were that the semis would be played over two legs and no team would be relegated for three years.

All four semi-finalists hailed from the south of England: Saracens, Harlequins, Wasps and Gloucester–Hartpury. The southern flavour to the table did raise questions of a north–south divide in the league with Nigel Melville confirming that the RFU would look at this. Whilst praise was heaped on the newly formed Loughborough Lightning outfit that eventually finished fifth in the table, Melville suggested that when the league was reviewed the authorities would not be afraid of debating drafting players in order to even out any geographical differences. However, at the time of writing this remained a discussion point rather than a proposed action.

The first semi-final saw Saracens, who finished top of the regular table, take on Gloucester–Hartpury who had finished fourth. The north London side were convincing winners across the two legs, coming away with a 62–0 victory on the road and then 45–26 at home. Meanwhile Harlequins, who finished second, played out two close matches with Wasps in third. Just six points separated the sides in the first leg, which Quins won 25–19, before upping the intensity to come away 22–7 winners in the second leg.

The very first Tyrrells Premier 15s final between the two London clubs would be played at the Ealing Trailfinders ground on Sunday 29 April. Although there wasn't a defending champion, Harlequins Ladies were the last club to lift the old Women's Premiership title. The match referee was Sarah Cox, England's highest-ranking female official, who had only recently returned from taking control of the Commonwealth Games Women's Rugby Sevens final on the Gold Coast.

We are delighted to be supporting Wooden Spoon and would like to thank everyone for their dedication and devotion. If you would like to find out more about Artemis, please contact your financial adviser, call 0800 092 2051 or visit artemisfunds.com.

ARTEMIS
The PROFIT Hunter

Tyrrells Premier 15s
Winners 2017/18

ABOVE Lotte Clapp of Saracens celebrates with her teammates after victory in the Tyrrells Premier 15s Final v. Harlequins Ladies.

Some 2,000 fans turned out for the fixture to see Saracens eventually prevail 24–20 in a closely fought seven-try battle. Both sides were flooded with international talent. Sarries included seven England stars in their starting XV and it will come as little surprise that the signing of Marlie Packer paid dividends for the victors as she put in a Player of the Match final performance.

Rob Cain had led his Saracens side to the inaugural title and he still struggles to explain his emotions on the day: 'I wouldn't do it justice in words but I just couldn't stop smiling I was so, so happy for the players and support staff. So much work goes into a season, let alone a championship-winning one. It was great to see their smiles and happiness after the final whistle.

'Every player and staff member has their own back story and it was great to see families, partners and friends all celebrate together. It was also many players' first senior rugby season and to see them celebrate was a great way to see all their hard work to come to fruition.'

After years invested into women's rugby in England, Cain has now become head coach of the USA women's side. His move into international rugby is a fillip for all English coaches as they are recognised and promoted on a global scale.

Following the end of the season Waterman also announced her retirement from international rugby. However, the 82-times-capped full back will continue playing for Wasps: 'I have loved being part of the Wasps squad and I am looking forward to playing without the pressure of also performing at international level. I also feel that I can really add to the Wasps team as a senior player. I enjoy working with the younger players, seeing them develop not only in the club but also through their opportunities with international rugby. The chance to play for the Barbarians is also something I would love to do.'

There have been suggestions that over the coming years the league could go professional, with match payments for players coming first. The RFU has said that they want the Tyrrells Premier 15s to grow steadily and avoid any club getting into financial difficulty by growing faster than its means.

As the league looks forward to its second season, the early success it has enjoyed is yet another marker in the rise of women's rugby, still the fastest-growing area of rugby union on the planet.

The Spirit of the Barbarians
STILL AS RELEVANT AS EVER

by CHRIS FOY

England just couldn't withstand or match the onslaught. It was a wondrous exhibition of audacious sporting skill and class and exuberance, bringing the victory it deserved.

Days before his team carried out their dazzling heist at Twickenham, Pat Lam was asked about the modern-day relevance of the Barbarians and whether he felt a responsibility to protect the entire concept. 'Without a doubt,' was the Bristol head coach's reply. He went on to articulate how the result mattered as much as other elements more associated with the invitational team: entertainment and daring play and forging multi-national bonds, often with the assistance of alcohol. 'We don't want to confuse the Barbarians' tradition as just coming together and having a good time,' said Lam. 'That's just the process to get the win.'

By the evening of Sunday 27 May, many missions had been accomplished. The Barbarians did win, at a time when every positive result wards off the continual threat to their status in a crowded rugby landscape. They also provided vivid, trademark entertainment, on the way to scoring nine tries – and more points than anyone had ever scored against England at their national stadium in the long history of the international game.

There was more. Their stunning 63–45 victory served as a launch-pad for Chris Ashton's renewed quest to revive his Test career. Within weeks of scoring a hat-trick for the Barbarians, the back-three flier had agreed to return home from Toulon, to sign for Sale – as a means of putting himself back into contention for a role at next year's World Cup.

On another personal note, it was a triumphant occasion for the visiting captain, Juan Martín Fernández Lobbe, the Argentine flanker who led the influential Toulon contingent also featuring two deadly Fijian runners who tore England's defence apart time and again – Semi Radradra and Josua Tuisova. Lam's squad wanted to give the captain a fitting send-off and they did just that, culminating in Fernández Lobbe striking the final conversion in an extension of his formidable repertoire.

That captured the essence of the occasion: successful fun. It was exactly what the Barbarians are supposed to be all about – and showed why they can remain relevant and alluring, rather than a fading, old-fashioned relic of the amateur era. All the miss-passes and off-loads, the side-steps and swallow-dives and whacky celebration routines are widely cherished within the game, but it is the scoreline which means that the frivolity is not hollow.

Lam worked wonders in a short space of time. Three years earlier, the Barbarians had come to Twickenham and been thrashed 73–12 by a scratch England side. Not this time. This time, they amounted to the sum of their considerable parts, despite staying true to the old-school values which required them to get acquainted in licensed premises around London.

The man in charge understood the need to let the players have some leeway and trust them still to deliver the goods. He grasped the culture so well, having ended his own playing career with the final try as the Barbarians came back from the dead against Wales in Cardiff back in 2002 – going from 25–0 down to winning 40–25, with a barnstorming second-half fight-back.

'The Barbarians are about the ethos and spirit of rugby,' said Lam, prior to a match which would further enhance his coaching pedigree. 'I personally believe it's the greatest team game where everybody's aspirations are dependent on their team-mates and the management. To achieve that it's about building relationships off the field so that you get that trust and ability to express yourself. If you don't have that, you're playing as individuals.

RIGHT Finn Russell of the Barbarians shares a joke with Chris Ashton during the victory over England, 27 May 2018.

'A lot of time is spent getting to know each other really well. We had a nice dinner last night and it was great – we were all around the one table. Some were on the wine, some were on the beer and some were on soft drinks. Most important is the chat and the connection. The beauty of this team is there are 12 countries represented, if you include me. Everyone was mingling and getting to know each other socially, many of them having played against each other this season.

ABOVE Barbarians' Chris Ashton scores the second of his three tries in the Ba-Ba's spectacular victory.

RIGHT Zach Mercer scores a first-half try for England.

'Some people misunderstand that it's just about going out and getting boozed up, but it's not. It's about being in a relaxed environment and being able to chat and have good conversations, and I mingled around as the boys were getting to know [each other] and talked to some of them and there was some unbelievable chat going on around more things than just rugby. That's great and it's why I love the game of rugby. That was what it was about before money got involved.'

Similar sentiments were expressed by Clermont's France hooker Benjamin Kayser in the aftermath of the remarkable result at Twickenham: that the Barbarians were a means for players to re-connect with the lost soul of their sport. It is a throw-back that they value – which is why so many household names still sign up. By the time Kayser was explaining this mind-set, it had become apparent that the preparations for beating England had been wildly unique.

Armed with so much talent, Lam had undertaken a delicate balancing act. Fierce work ethic collided with hearty socialising. A drone had been used to film training, for reasons of later recall. Asked how many sessions his team had, he said: 'It was three. It was funny because I said to them, "Fellas that was a really good training session but I know that some of you probably don't even remember it. But you can look at the pictures!"'

On the Thursday night before the Sunday game, the Barbarians had enjoyed a Seventies-themed fancy dress night out. Radradra and Tuisova were clad in disco outfits, accompanied by lurid wigs. Victor Vito, the ex-All Black number eight, wore a blond wig. Scotland fly-half Finn Russell dressed as Austin Powers. Justin Tipuric was the Cookie Monster. Chris Ashton was a hippy. It certainly didn't alleviate the mood of English dismay when these high-jinks came to light.

The try celebrations in a huddle and a special commemorative hand-shake were masterminded by the charismatic Clermont prop, Loni Uhila – a heavyweight boxer known as 'Tongan Bear'. He was the figurehead for the theatrical extras, but there was a serious side to the Barbarians' work too.

Again, Lam had struck just the right note. He showed his players familiar footage of the classic try against the All Blacks back in 1973, rounded off by Gareth Edwards, after the fuse was lit from deep by the fast feet of another Welshman, Phil Bennett. But what Lam sought to highlight was effort, not artistry. He froze the video to show how many men in black-and-white shirts chased back to their own 22 when New Zealand had kicked through.

The fundamental message was that graft would lead them to the glory-glory outcome they craved. When they weren't painting London red or singing along to party tunes on the team coach, that was the message that the players took to heart. When they did final training drills in the over-crowded car park of their hotel in Richmond on the morning of the game, that was what they kept in mind.

What followed was mesmeric. England were 21–0 down in the first 12 minutes; the victims of three stunning strikes. Lam had suggested that when he started planning for the fixture, while still on duty with Bristol late last season, he had realised that he would be engaging in 'fantasy rugby', given the array of firepower at his disposal. And so it proved.

Ashton, Radradra and Tuisova were all unstoppable forces – running around or straight through their opponents. Up front, Vito showed his athletic class, as he does so often for La Rochelle, while Justin Tipuric revelled in the open spaces. One try by the visitors, rounded off by Sitaleki Timani, contained more off-loads than some sides manage in a season.

England just couldn't withstand or match the onslaught, despite some flash moves of their own. It was one of those occasions when the crowd are willing on the home team, but can still revel in the razzmatazz which is occurring at their expense. It was a wondrous exhibition of audacious sporting skill and class and exuberance, bringing the victory it deserved.

The aftermath was dominated by local concerns about a fourth successive English defeat, but Lam's men were showered in bouquets too, for laying on a spectacle and taking steps to preserve a valued, endangered concept. As a sign of how the wind was blowing, Sir Clive Woodward's criticism of the annual 'circus', as he described the established end-of-season fixture, led to a social media backlash against the World Cup-winning ex-England coach.

What the response made clear was that there is still space at the top end of an increasingly saturated sport for what the Barbarians represent. There is still space for a team who can meet five days earlier, train just three times – often hung over, party in Seventies gear … and then go out and beat a strong England team on their home patch at Twickenham.

ABOVE Barbarians' Fijian wing Josua Tuisova, an Olympic Sevens gold medallist, keeps a move going with an improvised pass.

RIGHT Juan Martín Fernández Lobbe kicks the final conversion.

2

INTERNATIONAL SCENE

Brave Blossoms Rising
JAPAN AND THE WORLD CUP

by RAECHELLE INMAN

'We are starting to build exactly the type of character we need in preparation for the World Cup. I believe we can achieve something great next year.'

It was one of the biggest upsets in the history of rugby: Japan beat South Africa in the 2015 Rugby World Cup 34–32. The two-time world champions were humiliated by the Brave Blossoms. The Japanese side were sensational from the outset. And even though the Springboks scored four tries to three, Japan always looked the better outfit.

In the closing moments of the dramatic match Japan's brave captain, New Zealand-born Michael Leitch, turned down a potential equalising kick at goal to press on for glory. One surge went to the video referee but there was no conclusive evidence, leaving a fellow native Kiwi, replacement wing Karne Hesketh to score a sensational try in the corner to secure the unbelievable victory for Japan in the 84th minute and set the ground at Brighton in England alight.

The coach of the Japanese side at the time, Australian Eddie Jones, said before the match that if his side won the scrum battle they could go on and win the match. No one thought twice about his comments but they were insightful and he certainly prepared the squad with an effective strategy, fitness, precision and most importantly razor-sharp execution.

ABOVE Japan's captain Michael Leitch is tackled by Tommaso Castello of Italy during their first meeting in the summer of 2018, in Oita, Japan. Japan won 34–17.

LEFT Kenki Fukuoka can't quite break free during the first Italy Test, Oita, 9 June 2018.

There were so many physical mismatches evident across the park on that sunny day on the south coast of Britain. The only way the Japanese could win was to play in unison, and at pace. The speed with which they moved the ball was captivating and was matched by constant support and great hands. The Boks always looked as though they would pull away, but each time the Japanese, playing in harmony and with an inventive style, managed calmly to claw their way back. And eventually achieve a famous triumph.

Since shocking the rugby world on that fateful day how has the team progressed and matured? Current coach, New Zealand's Jamie Joseph, says: 'different players, different game – it's all different'.

One big difference for the team will be playing at home for Rugby World Cup 2019. The ninth World Cup will be played in 12 venues across the whole of Japan. Home support should provide a great lift for the team, given the passion of the Japanese crowds. Joseph hopes hosting will be a 'positive advantage' for his side.

The logo for the 2019 tournament is based on the theme of 'unity'. As a completely new territory for the tournament to be held in, Japan will become one with the players and fans from the leading rugby nations of the world, working towards the common goal of making rugby a truly global sport. The host cities across the country will be inspired to make the tournament an unforgettable one and will stand together to welcome and entertain fans from all over the globe. The new RWC emblem integrates the rising sun and Mount Fuji with the World Rugby logo; it represents Japan and the world coming together in the name of rugby.

Joseph is uniquely placed to guide the Brave Blossoms. He played provincial rugby for Otago and went on to represent the All Blacks, debuting in 1992 and remaining a regular starter until 1995 when he formed part

LEFT Jamie Joseph enjoys his post-match press conference after the Sunwolves' 26–23 Super Rugby win over the Stormers in Hong Kong in May 2018. Joseph coaches the Sunwolves as well as the Japan national team.

RIGHT Akihito Yamada and Kazuki Himeno (20, who finally got the touchdown) of Japan combine for the third try of Japan's 28–0 win over Georgia in June 2018.

of the World Cup squad that lost to South Africa in the final. He then moved to Japan, playing for the Fukuoka Sanix Blues for six years, which saw him selected for the Japanese national side ahead of the 1999 World Cup. He debuted on 1 May 1999 against Canada in Tokyo.

He retired in 2001 and turned his attention to coaching back in New Zealand. After making his way through the coaching ranks, including a spell as head coach of the Maori All Blacks, he was named coach of the Otago Highlanders for the 2011 Super Rugby series. His coaching peaked with the Highlanders defeating the Hurricanes 21–14 in the Super Rugby final in Wellington in 2015. The position as head coach of Japan is his first stint as a national coach.

No stranger to living in Japan, the coach loves the cultural differences, citing, 'food, safety, efficiency and friends' as his highlights. The Japanese side is traditionally the strongest rugby union power in Asia, having participated in every RWC tournament since 1987.

His proudest moment coaching the Japanese national side to date was preparing the team that drew 23–23 with France in Paris in November 2017, adding 'If we had won all three Tests recently against Italy and Georgia that would have been an achievement as well.'

Joseph thinks that the inclusion of a team in Super Rugby has benefited the national side. 'It has accelerated development – created belief and valuable experiences playing some of the best players in the world, mental resilience around playing in a tough competition with travel and absence from family.'

He believes that the squad is tracking well in preparation for RWC 2019. 'We are getting there now – coaching the Sunwolves gives me more time with the players; winning three drawing one and losing one out of the last five Test matches is a good sign. But we have limited depth in Japan so we will need luck to avoid injuries along the way,' Joseph said.

'In the build-up to next year's World Cup I am focussed on building a positive team culture, creating belief in our game that we can beat tier one sides – having a professional mind-set given that the game is still amateur in Japan,' he added.

As he was in 2015 we can expect skipper Michael Leitch to be outstanding for the red and whites, along with fly half Yu Tamura and number eight Yamanaki Mafi. The young players to watch out for are full backs Ryuji Noguchi and Rikiya Matsuda and blindside flanker Kazuki Himeno.

Ensuring an optimal mix of home-grown and foreign players is key to success. 'I will pick the best players available who align with right rugby skill-sets and character,' Joseph says, adding that preparing to peak at the right time for the big games involves 'steady progress, a balance of rest and training, and competitive matches. Alignment between coaches and players and improved leadership are critical too.'

The Kiwi considers his team capable of making history by reaching the quarter-final at next year's Rugby World Cup.

The 2019 tournament hosts thrashed Georgia 28–0 in June, completing a busy month of home Tests with a second victory after splitting a two-match series with Italy.

It was the first time Japan had held a side ranked in the world's top 12 scoreless, but it was the character shown by the Brave Blossoms in bouncing back from their second Test loss to Italy that ignited hope from Joseph.

'During the Italy Tests we showed glimpses of our brand of rugby – players executing with confidence and making great decisions,' the former All Black told reporters. 'But the Georgia Test showed the commitment and

GREENE KING

IPA
INDIA PALE ALE

PROUD PARTNER OF
WOODEN SPOON

GREENE KING IPA
THE PERFECT
MATCH PINT

ABOVE Ryuji Noguchi of the Sunwolves looks for a way through the Waratahs defence, Super Rugby, 7 July 2018, Sydney.

alignment of the team, and we are starting to build exactly the type of character we need in preparation for the World Cup,' added Joseph, who tipped his side to 'achieve something great' next year.

'If we make the last eight it would be a great achievement and I do think we are on track – if the players are willing to put their bodies on the line. My job is to find a way to win, to find a way to create confidence for the players.'

Jamie Joseph will measure the success of his tenure as coach of Japan by building 'a great brand of rugby – smart rugby players playing with purpose, pride, skill, toughness – never giving in and having fun'.

The fact that an amateur rugby minnow like Japan can slay a giant like South Africa is just the kind of excitement rugby fans want from RWC 2019. Rugby's survival as a global code of football can only be enhanced by a Japanese team playing well in a home World Cup.

One thing guaranteed is that no rugby super-power will ever go into a match up with the Brave Blossoms complacent because everyone knows what they are capable of.

After Thirty Years
WORLD CUP QUALIFIERS

by CHRIS THAU

Refereeing rows, player eligibility disputes, underdog victories and one team's 30-year quest to qualify for a first appearance at the Rugby World Cup finals. Qualifying for RWC 2019 had it all.

The newly born Rugby World Cup tournament was barely a year old when the IRFB (as World Rugby was then titled) decided to drop the original by-invitation format for the second tournament to be hosted by the then Five Nations – England, Scotland, Ireland, Wales and France – in 1991. On 4 November 1988 the IRFB confirmed that the eight quarter-finalists of the previous tournament, New Zealand, France, Wales, Australia, Scotland, England, Ireland and Fiji would automatically qualify for the 1991 RWC and that a qualifying system would be set in place to enable the other 29 IRFB unions to compete for the remaining eight slots. The distribution secured three entries for qualifiers from the Americas, two for Europe, two for Asia/Oceania and one for Africa. It was also agreed that existing competition structures would be used whenever possible to avoid duplication, as well as save time and money, and that South Africa was not going to be invited.

Not long after all the information was made public, the Asian Championship, identified as one of the existing regional tournaments to be used as a RWC qualifying round, kicked off in Hong Kong on 12 November 1988. In the inaugural match, the first ever RWC qualifying tie, the hosts Hong Kong tackled Sri Lanka, winning 45–3, at the HK Government Stadium. The final of the tournament, which acted as the first round of the Asia/Oceania

zone, had an unexpected outcome, with a fired-up Korea defeating Japan 17–13. With Hong Kong finishing third, Japan and Korea qualified for round two, which also included RWC newcomers Western Samoa and Tonga, a veteran of the 1987 tournament.

Thirty years later, almost to the day, the Hong Kong team, having hovered on the fringes of the RWC qualifying process for three decades, has now reached the final hurdle, the quadrangular RWC Repechage Tournament in Marseille, France, that will determine the 20th participating nation in Japan 2019. The work of the ambitious Hong Kong RFU has paid off, with the national team reaching the repechage stage undefeated. Captained by lock forward James Cunningham, Hong Kong defeated both Asian contenders South Korea and Malaysia, home and away, to finish top of the ARFU Championship table with 19 championship points, scoring 227 points and conceding 44. The away match against the Koreans at Incheon proved to be the toughest challenge for coach Leigh Jones' men, as the Koreans, coached by Choi Chang-ryul, gave a good account of themselves, losing 21–30, yet outscoring the visitors by three tries to two. In the play-off against Cook Islands, the Oceania runner-up, who had reached the play-off at the expense of Tahiti, disqualified for using two ineligible players, Hong Kong were equally ruthless scoring an aggregate of 77 points to 3 in their two matches.

Perhaps, in different circumstances, winning a qualifying zone would have been enough to take a team directly to the finals of the RWC 2019 tournament optimistically named 'Rugby comes to Asia'. But this did not happen in the qualifying rounds of RWC 2019. With Japan appointed as hosts, the zone's second best (called Asia 1) might have been granted a starting position among the 20-strong finalists, and even perhaps host a pool or a couple of matches. Instead, it was felt, probably, that such a qualifying process would not be demanding enough, hence the current format, involving in addition to Hong Kong, Canada, Germany and the runner-up in the Africa zone (Africa 2), confirmed as this book was about to go to press as Kenya.

The astonishing progress of Hong Kong to a potential RWC participant has been the result of an eight-year process of extensive development, which commenced in 2008, explains Dai Rees, the HK RFU Chief Rugby Operations Officer. This is clearly reflected in the current World Rugby ranking of 21st, the highest of the four repechage-participating Unions. In order to implement his programme, Rees, whose rugby CV as a head coach includes Gwent Dragons, Wales Women, Wales U20s, Wales U19s and Wales Sevens teams, has surrounded himself by a group of capable and dedicated rugby professionals, who have in common a perfectionist desire to see Hong Kong doing well on the Asian and world stage. Rees' right-hand man is another well-known Welsh coach, Leigh Jones, who is currently the head coach of the HK team, having spent two years with Eddie Jones

ABOVE Hong Kong's dynamic Cado Lee Ka-To is tackled by a smiling Cook Islands giant in the final Asia/Oceania RWC play-off.

and Japan up to the last World Cup. Jones' assistant with the national team is Andrew Hall, who is also running the Elite Rugby Programme, supported by four Premiership Club Coaching Officers.

Rees explained: 'From the outset, it was clear that if we were to improve at international level we needed to work closely with our six Premiership clubs, creating a high performance mind-set both on and off the field, while also introducing a stricter HK eligibility quota for each club to ensure our HK-born players were playing at the top level in our domestic game. To their credit the Union approved the plan and in order to drive and support it they centrally funded a Director of Rugby/Head Coach for each of the Premiership Clubs, who in addition to their club jobs, work with all our national squads at both senior and junior level – Joe Shaw (now at Saracens), Craig Hammond, Andrew Hall, Mark Fatilofa (all current HK men's XV.) All this was initially supported by a high-performance scholarship scheme with national players required to train with our programmes four or five times a week. This was achievable because Hong Kong is geographically so small that all central training locations are within easy reach.

'In parallel with the senior domestic development we restructured our national age-grade programmes with an emphasis on both skill and physical development. This system took three to four years to implement and it is paying dividends now as it has allowed us to qualify for the last five World Junior Trophy tournaments from a tiny player base. It has also meant that our players are ready for senior international selection at a younger age, for example Max Denmark at 18, Finn Field 20, Mike Parfitt 20 or Alex Post a former U20s captain.

'Alongside these initiatives we worked in partnership with the HK Institute of Sport to create for the first time a full-time rugby programme for our players. This was achieved following our first Asian Games silver medal in 2010, which opened up a considerable funding stream from the HK Government, for players, coaches and support staff, which enabled us to set in place our first full-time rugby programme for men and women at both sevens and XVs. The next step, in conjunction with all stakeholders, was the launch of the full-time Elite Rugby Programme in 2015.'

The Rees blueprint has the full support of the HKRFU Board of Directors, as the CEO Robbie McRobbie explained: 'Hong Kong, as "Asia's World City", has a diverse community and our aim is to provide a pathway for all through to national representation – Chinese and non-ethnic Chinese alike. Our men's and women's national teams include Caucasian and Eurasian players whose families have lived in Hong Kong for three or more generations, and conversely Chinese players whose parents arrived more recently from Mainland China – this is the melting pot that Hong Kong has always been. Everyone here is an immigrant it's just a question of when you arrived!

'For young people in Hong Kong having role models they can identify with and strive to emulate is desirable, and in that regard international players like Salom Yiu Kam-shing and Cado Lee Ka-to are important role models. Salom was the product of the HKRU youth development programme and came from a government secondary school in the New Territories – he has gone on to become a standing feature in both our national sevens and XVs teams. Cado has recently returned from a season playing with the NEC Green Rockets in the Japan Top League, demonstrating his ability to compete at the highest level of professional rugby. Our performances in the qualifying rounds so far have been tremendous, and if we manage to make it to the finals of RWC 2019 in Japan, this could be our third RWC tournament to date after the Women's XV who played in last year's WRWC and with the men's Sevens team playing in the Sevens RWC in San Francisco – which is not too bad for a small union like ours.'

If Hong Kong, better known as the host of a famous Sevens tournament than for their exploits in the 15-a-side game, qualify for Japan 2019, which is a distinct possibility, they will be drawn in Pool B alongside World Champions New Zealand, South Africa, Italy and Namibia, winner of the Africa zone (Africa 1), after their victory in the Africa Gold Cup was completed in August 2018. With hosts Japan playing in Pool A, this would be the first time two Asian nations have competed in a RWC tournament.

Chaos in Europe

The presence of Germany at the repechage tournament at the end of a long and tortuous process is in itself a minor miracle, given the utter pandemonium that has engulfed German rugby since September 2017, when the contract between the German Union (DRV) and its main sponsor, the Wild Rugby foundation, came to an end. This was followed by allegations of match fixing and of illegal use of ineligible players by three of the unions involved in the Rugby Europe Championship.

In the autumn of 2017, the disagreements between German Union officials and Dr Hans-Peter Wild, the sponsor of the Wild Rugby Academy, of Heidelberg Ruderklub, and of the German national team, as well as the new owner of the Stade Français club, led to a complete breakdown in relations, with the international players from Ruderklub and their coach Kobus Potgeiter going on strike. In a press statement issued in January 2018 the DRV blamed Wild and his company for the breakdown and announced that it had hired former Uruguay coach Pablo Lemoine and Australians Paul Healy and Chris Lane to work with the national team. By that time Germany, deprived of its best players, was struggling in the Rugby Europe Championship, having been demolished by all its First Division opponents: 64–0 by Georgia, 69–15 by Belgium, 84–10 by Spain and 85–6 by Romania. The argument surrounding Wild, whose uncle Georg played for Germany and father Rudolf, a rowing Olympian, played for Ruderklub, engulfed the entirety of German rugby, and eventually the DRV President Klaus Blank resigned at an acrimonious extraordinary general meeting in Hannover at the end of January. Promptly the German Federation recommenced negotiations with Wild and his team, which included Robert Mohr, a former captain of La Rochelle and German international, and former DRV vice-president in charge of 15-a-side rugby Hans-Joachim Wallenwein, who had been sidelined by the previous administration. Meanwhile the players' strike ended the way it started, that is without much ado, and coaches, Lemoine and Potgeiter, like good rugby men, started working together to salvage what was left of a shambolic season.

Meanwhile, as the German crisis was inching towards resolution, the entire qualifying process in Europe was thrown into disarray by a series of eligibility disputes, as well as by allegations of refereeing bias. A few months earlier it looked as if Romania, one of the 1987 RWC originals, were calmly heading towards their ninth

consecutive RWC tournament appearance. But then they lost to Spain 22–10 in Madrid in February and suddenly *Los Leones* became the front-runner for Japan 2019. The absence of a TMO in Spain's match with Russia was a minor controversy which gathered momentum when the Spanish players, angered by what they perceived as a biased performance by referee Vlad Iordachescu in their unexpected 18–10 defeat by Belgium, attacked the Romanian official, who had to be defended by the Belgian players, at the end of the match. The defeat of Spain offered Romania a lifeline in their race to qualify as Europe 1 (Georgia was an automatic qualifier) so it looked as if they would be joining Ireland, Scotland, Japan and Samoa, the winner of the Europe/Oceania play-off, in Pool A of RWC 2019. Meanwhile the Spanish Federation, which had tried several times to convince Rugby Europe to change the referee before the Belgium match, approached World Rugby asking for a review and an investigation of the match and its circumstances. That was duly granted and, having reviewed the match, World Rugby felt that the Spanish complaint about the referee had some merit and recommended replaying the fixture, advice which they subsequently withdrew.

But then all hell broke loose when a Russian researcher detected that Romania's Tongan-born centre Sione Faka'osilea had made an appearance for his country of birth in a sevens match – which rendered him ineligible for Romania. The revelation opened a can of worms, which, in addition to Romania, sucked in both Spain and Belgium on charges of various eligibility infringements. The Romanian Federation lodged an appeal, rightly observing that the Tongan Union had confirmed in writing that Faka'osilea was eligible to play for Romania. The Spanish also produced documentation that showed that they had checked the eligibility of their French-born players in good faith. But that was not enough for the Independent Disputes Committee appointed by World Rugby, who acknowledged that there was no malice in the mistakes that allowed ineligible players to get selected but nevertheless penalised the three federations, Romania, Spain and Belgium. The fact that all three have been found guilty of at worst negligence, rather than of dishonestly breaking the law, points to the eligibility regulation as the likely culprit. Given the massive impact of an eligibility infringement, the absence of a standardised validation procedure to double-check an application, supervised and approved by World Rugby, is indeed surprising.

The WR ruling had far-reaching consequences, which saw Russia climbing to the top of the Rugby Europe tree, as Europe 1, with Germany as the runner-up. So, with Russia (now coached by Lyn Jones, formerly of Newport Dragons) qualified for RWC 2019, the German team, coached now by the duo Pablo Lemoine and Kobus Potgeiter, carried on in their quest to reach Japan in 2019. The German side managed to recapture a modicum of form just in time, having to deal with a determined Portugal team in the final European zone play-off. They narrowly prevailed 16–13 in a finely balanced encounter, after trailing *Los Lobos* at half time, thanks

RIGHT Russia *v.* Spain, February 2018. The match score was 20–13 to Spain, but that was before the player eligibility row. The Russian front row (from left) are Andrey Volkov, Stanislav Selskyi and Andrey Polivanov.

LEFT Mathieu Ducau of Germany is challenged by Jack Lam of Samoa during their RWC qualifying match on 14 July 2018 in Heidelberg.

to the accurate kicking of their South African-born centre Raynor Parkinson, who landed three penalties and a conversion, unlike the Portuguese kicker, Louis Rodriguez, who missed three out of his six kicks at goal. As expected, Germany lost both their home and away play-off matches against Samoa. But while there was very little to appreciate in their 10-try, 61–15 drubbing at Apia Park in the away game, there was plenty of guts, aptitude and rugby in their 42–28 home defeat at Heidelberg – having led 28–21 some 15 minutes before the end. Their competent, albeit inconsistent, performance must have given Lemoine and Potgeiter a glimmer of hope that the shortcomings exposed in Heidelberg could be ironed out by the time they reach Marseille in November, to enable Germany to challenge for the remaining RWC starting slot in Pool B.

Africa and Canada

Which African team would qualify as of right and which would get a second chance in the repechage tournament was decided by Rugby Africa's top-level championship, the six-nation Gold Cup, which was still being played as this article was being drafted. After three rounds, Kenya, coached by New Zealander Ian Snook (Kenya's previous coach Jerome Paarwater of South Africa was unceremoniously sacked after five years in charge, just before the end of 2017) and Namibia, coached by former Wales lock forward Phil Davies, were both unbeaten, with three wins out of three matches each. Namibia, however, had three bonus-point wins, while Kenya had no bonuses. Kenya made sure of at least second place with a penultimate round 67–0 thrashing of Tunisia but needed a convincing win in the last-round decider with Namibia, away in Windhoek, to grab the coveted Africa 1 place. It was not to be. Namibia had too much forward power and tactical control and Kenya's lively backs had too few opportunities. Kenya scored the first try early on but Namibia pulled away in the last quarter and eventually won comfortably 53–28. Namibia's reward is to join New Zealand, South Africa and Italy in Pool B in Japan; Kenya will go to the repechage.

The fourth participant in the November repechage tournament is Canada, another one of the hand-picked teams of the 1987 RWC, now going through a major existential crisis that saw them fail to reach the RWC as Americas 1 for the first time. They lost their long-serving head-coach, former All Black full back Kieran Crowley in January 2016. His fellow New Zealander Mark Anscombe did not last long, as he was fired after the 52–16 defeat (eight US tries to Canada's one) at the hands of the US Eagles, in San Diego, on 1 July 2017, having drawn the home leg 28–28 in Hamilton, Ontario on 24 June. It was claimed that Anscombe, who had coached New Zealand U20 and Ulster prior to the Canadian job, had lost the dressing room for saying that too many of the Canadian players were not playing at a high enough level and they were not conditioned for the demands of international rugby. He was also quoted as saying that the Canadian system was broken and pointing out that there was no centre of excellence to help fast-track players to the national teams. Although many of the issues identified by Anscombe are being addressed by Rugby Canada, the new Canada coach Kingsley Jones, who joined Rugby Canada in October 2017, immediately became aware of the limited amount of game-time the Canadian professionals experience before international matches.

'Basically the skill levels and playing standards in the domestic amateur Canadian game are pretty low, which is a fact of life. However, a big problem is that the majority of the overseas-based professionals, with the exception of Jeff Hassler [then of Ospreys], do not get enough play-time with their teams. In this respect a revealing indicator of where Canada are at this moment is that from the November Test series to the February RWC qualifiers versus Uruguay, Hassler was the only player in the team to start in more than one game. There were

guys in the Canadian team who had hardly played in a game, which does not help at all when your first match of the season is a Test,' observed Jones, who coached Russia in RWC 2011.

With Jones at the helm Canada lost the home qualifier against Uruguay, coached by Argentine Esteban Meneses, 29–38 but came within two points of an upset when they lost 32–31 in Montevideo. In seven years they dropped 10 places in the World Rugby rankings from 12 in 2011 to 22. Will Canada be able to sort out its perceived shortcomings to be able to win the repechage stage and return to the RWC fold? A challenging question, given the fact that no one knows for sure how good in fact Hong Kong are, except that at the moment they are the highest placed of the four participants in World Rugby rankings (21st), or whether Germany (currently the lowest at 29th; Kenya are 28th) could make a significant quality jump to be able to challenge such strong opponents. There is no doubt that Jones will leave no stone unturned in his desire to see the Canadians reaching top form by November. He knows what it takes to reach the RWC finals, but so does Lemoine, who both played and coached at RWC tournaments. The same could said about Dai Rees and his lieutenant Leigh Jones who are carefully plotting the progress of the former colony. Without doubt the Repechage 2018 will be a fascinating tournament.

Final Day Drama
THE HSBC WR SEVENS SERIES

by **PAUL BOLTON**

'This was such a memorable series. We feel for Fiji, who came charging and overhauled us with three tournaments to go, only to come up short in Paris, but that is sport for you.'

South Africa retained their title on a dramatic final day at the Stade Jean-Bouin in Paris where their victory over England in the final meant heartbreak for Fiji. The 24–14 win in the very last match of the series gave South Africa only their second tournament victory of the season compared to Fiji's five but it was reward for their overall consistency over the 10-tournament campaign.

Fiji went to Paris as favourites to win the series after they had beaten South Africa 21–17 in the London final at Twickenham the previous week to claim their fourth consecutive tournament victory, after successes in Vancouver, Hong Kong and Singapore. But Fiji came unstuck against England, who were to play the role of kingmakers, in the quarter-finals in Paris. A last gasp try from Tom Mitchell, which rounded off an exhilarating 26-pass move, secured a 19–17 win in an epic contest.

England's win left the door ajar for the Blitzboks, who also needed a late try, scored by Justin Geduld, to snatch a jittery 15–10 victory over spirited Spain to reach the semi-finals. Two tries from Dewald Human then saw off New Zealand in the semi-final, while Fiji kept up the pressure by beating Ireland and the USA to claim fifth place in Paris and leave South Africa requiring victory over England to overhaul their seven-point lead.

SERIES CHAMPIONS 2018

An early try from Werner Kok was cancelled out by tries from Ollie Lindsay-Hague and Dan Norton. Ryan Oosthuizen pulled South Africa level again before Human secured the important third try and Justin Geduld added a penalty – the last of just five kicked during the season – to bring the series to a thrilling finale.

South Africa finished with 182 points, two ahead of Fiji with New Zealand, who took bronze in Paris, third with 150 points.

'This was such a memorable series. We feel for Fiji, who came charging and overhauled us with three tournaments to go, only to come up short in Paris, but that is sport for you,' said South Africa coach Neil Powell. 'We kept the focus on ourselves and what we wanted to achieve as a squad and a system. We were graced and blessed as it worked out for us in the end.'

South Africa's first back-to-back series win made up for the disappointment of finishing fourth in the Commonwealth Games which, with the Sevens World Cup in July, meant their player base was increased to 28.

'We had this plan because of the three big events this year and realised that player management would be key,' Powell said. 'Unfortunately we let ourselves down at the Commonwealth Games where we finished fourth, so winning the series was a welcome reward.'

Powell was also rewarded by being voted Capgemini Men's Coach of the Series but only one of his players, Dylan Sage, made the HSBC Dream Team. Fiji provided four of the Dream Team – Kalione Nasoko, Jerry Tuwai, Amenoni Nasilasila and Eroni Sau – with Kenya's Oscar Ouma and Australia's Ben O'Donnell completing the line up.

Sau became the second Fijian to win the Rookie of the Year Award with Canada's Juston Douglas picking up the DHL Impact Player Award. Douglas did not win any of the individual awards during the series but his consistency across the season earned him 386 points, six more than O'Donnell.

Carlin Isles of the USA finished as the leading try-scorer in the series with 49, five clear of Luke Morgan of Wales with Canada's Nathan Hirayama topping the points table with 334, 18 more than Nasilasila. Over the series 17,028 points were scored with 2,715 tries and 1,714 conversions – 98 of them from Hirayama.

Ireland made a welcome return to the series after a 14-year absence although their participation was limited to appearances in London in Paris. But Ireland showed sufficient promise to hint at a bright future in this

format as they finished third at Twickenham where they were beaten only by Australia in their pool. Ireland upset the USA in the quarter-finals before going down 38–12 to Fiji in the semis. They took the bronze medal by surprising England, who were beaten by South Africa in their semi-final, in the third place play-off where Mark Roche's conversion of Jordan Conroy's last minute try clinched a 21–19 win.

Ireland topped their pool in Paris but were beaten by Canada in the quarter-finals and by Fiji in the semi-finals of the fifth-place play-off. Their haul of 27 series points was still one more than Russia, who competed in

all tournaments, and who were relegated as the lowest placed of the 20 core teams. Russia will be replaced by Japan for the 2018–19 series.

But England dropped from second to fifth in a mixed season which included a forgettable visit to Hong Kong for Simon Amor's team. England beat only South Korea in their pool and then went down 33–10 to Samoa in the 13th-place play-off. They finished joint 15th with South Korea and had just the one series point to show for their weekend in their former colony. Dan Norton helped to lift some of the gloom for England by scoring 38 tries in the series to take his career aggregate to 299, 28 ahead of Kenya's Collins Injera, the man whose record he took in 2017.

NEXUS

Moving business over the line

As specialist healthcare and education industry advisers and investors we provide a range of business and management services, including:

- Property fund management
- Real estate advisory services
- Corporate finance advice
- Private equity services
- International Opera Awards
- Investor Publishing: HealthInvestor UK, HealthInvestor Asia and EducationInvestor Global
- Code Hospitality community

For more information visit:

nexusgroup.co.uk | phpgroup.co.uk
healthinvestor.co.uk | healthinvestorasia.com
operaawards.org | educationinvestor.co.uk
codehospitality.co.uk

Property Management

Corporate Finance

Media

NEXUS

WE GO FURTHER

ABOVE Sara Goss of New Zealand receives the best player of the final award at the Paris Sevens from former France international Thomas Castaignède.

Kenya finished a creditable eighth with a record haul of 104 points but their coach, Innocent Simiyu, was sacked on their return home following a dispute over unpaid salaries. Simiyu accepted responsibility for Kenya's players concealing the branding of their shirt sponsor in Paris. Following protests from the players, Simiyu, a former Kenya captain, was reinstated by the Ministry of Sports, Culture and Heritage, which promised to work closely with the Kenya Rugby Union to resolve the pay dispute.

The sixth World Rugby HSBC Women's Sevens series was less controversial but also went down to the wire with Australia pipping New Zealand by two points despite losing to them, 33–7, in the final in Paris.

Australia gained early momentum by winning the first two of the five tournaments in Dubai and Sydney although New Zealand, the defending champions, won the other three in Kitakuyshu in Japan, Langford in Canada and Paris. But New Zealand's 14–12 defeat by the USA in Dubai was to prove costly. They finished fifth in the series opener and conceded an early eight-point advantage to Australia who never finished outside the top three.

Australia needed to reach the final in Paris to clinch the series – and their second title – and they got there with a thrilling 21–17 victory over the hosts. New Zealand booked their place in the final with a 34–7 win over Canada in the first semi-final but they then had to watch as France led 17–14 until Emilee Cherry scored from long range and late on to clinch the title for Australia.

New Zealand's Alan Bunting was voted Capgemini Women's Coach of the Series while Portia Woodman of the Black Ferns finished as leading try-scorer with 43 and her team-mate Michaela Blyde took the DHL Impact Player Award. Blyde finished the series with 229 points, having made 58 tackles, 44 breaks, 20 off-loads and 107 carries. She finished eight points clear of Japan's Chiharu Nakamura.

Woodman and Blyde were also included in the HSBC Dream Team along with Australia's Evania Pelite and Emma Tonegato, Russia's Baizat Khamidova, Spain's Patricia García and France's Montserrat Amédée. Amédée's team-mate Coralie Bertrand won the Rookie of the Year Award having helped France reach their first-ever cup final in Kitakyushu.

The women's series will expand further in 2018–19 with Infinity Park in Glendale, Colorado, hosting the first of the six tournaments.

New Hope for Les Bleus
THE WR U20 CHAMPIONSHIP

by ALAN LORIMER

This was a French squad packed with talented players and (worryingly for their opponents) about half are young enough to come back to contest the 2019 championship.

To quote *La Marseillaise*: '*Le jour de gloire est arrivé!*' 17 June 2018, to be precise, was the day that France secured their first ever Rugby World Under-20 title after defeating England 33–25 at a packed Stade de la Méditerranée in Béziers to inject a new spirit into the French game. The ramification of this momentous victory was summed up by *L'Équipe* newspaper which declared: '*Enfin un vent de fraîcheur et d'enthousiasme dans le climat morose du rugby français.*'

The last time that hope sprang anew like this for French rugby was in 2006 when France won what was to be the last Under-21 World Championship with a 24–13 victory over South Africa at Clermont-Ferrand, a match that will be remembered for the prodigious goal-kicking of Lionel Bauxis – six penalties and two drops. And it was a title win that was to spawn notable international careers for the likes of Guirado, Ouedraogo, Mermoz and Chouly.

This first ever World Rugby Under-20 Championship title for *Les Bluets* is surely an endorsement of the French academy system and perhaps sends a signal to the wealthy club owners that splashing the cash on ready-made foreign imports is not the only route to success. This was a French squad packed with talented players and (worryingly for their opponents) about half are young enough to come back to contest the 2019 championship. Fly half, Louis Carbonel, the Toulon-based playmaker, who just about equalled the feat of Bauxis by kicking 23 points in the final, headed a list of exciting backs, that included the skipper and scrum half, Arthur Coville, centre and poster boy Romain Ntamack, full back Clement Laporte and winger Matthis Lebel.

In the forwards, the stand-outs were back rows Cameron Woki and the 17-year-old sensation Jordan Joseph, plus the muscular 125-kg prop, Demba Bamba, whose front-row cohorts were not exactly featherweights either.

The France team was a balanced blend of formidable scrummaging front rows, powerful ball-carrying back-five forwards and skilful and pacy backs that ultimately proved irresistible. Yet the *Tricolores'* modest start to their title quest did little to enhance their championship credentials. In their opening round match against Ireland, *Les Bluets* trailed 5–17 at half time before scraping a 26–24 win. Then, against Georgia, France had to work hard for their 24–12 result.

Only in their final pool match against South Africa did France really show their title-winning potential by establishing a 36–7 lead at the break. The Junior Boks did hit back in the second half but the damage had been done early on and in the end France were comfortable winners by 46–29.

France duly finished top of their pool to join England, New Zealand and South Africa in the semi-finals. *Les Bluets'* task in the penultimate round was to topple the 2017 champions New Zealand, who had graduated from the pool stage with customary ease.

New Zealand have won the under-20 title more often than any other country and consequently there is an expectation of success. There was a feeling, however, that the 2018 Baby Blacks were lacking the X-factor that had made their championship-winning sides, and notably the 2017 group, such stand-out teams. That said the Baby Blacks had quality players in wing Caleb Clark, fly-half Harry Plummer and back row Tom Christie.

In the event New Zealand, despite defending heroically, were out-powered by the muscular French forwards even if *Les Bluets'* 3–0 half time lead barely

RIGHT France's Cameron Woki proves more than a handful for a pair of would-be English tacklers in the final.

reflected the balance of the game. The dividend, however, was delivered after the break when a try by Ntamack and the kicking of Carbonel gave the French side a 16–7 win and a place in the final against England.

For their part England, who have been by far the most successful country since 2013 in the under-20 championship, came through the pool stage with wins over Argentina, Italy and Scotland to secure their semi-final place against South Africa. In the penultimate round match at Narbonne, England looked comfortably en route to the final when they led the Junior Boks 22–7 at the break with tries from Tom Parton, Tom Hardwick, Ben White and seven points from the boot of the precocious talent that is Marcus Smith, South Africa responding with Sazi Sandi's converted score.

In a thrilling second half South Africa, who had to play without their quality fly-half, Damian Willemse, recovered ground with scores from Muller Uys and Ruan Nortje but an opportunist try by Jordan Olowofela, and the conversion by Smith gave England a 32–19 lead. In a frantic finish South Africa scored tries by Manuel Rass and Asenathi Ntlabakanye but not enough to prevent a 31–32 defeat.

For England it was a sixth consecutive opportunity to contest the under-20 final and to add to their title wins in 2013, 2014 and 2016. But against the physicality of the French forwards and a hard-hitting defence England were on the back foot for most of the first half largely due to *Les Bleus*' dominance at the scrum and what now seems the default position of referees to award a penalty when the weaker scrum is shoved backwards.

Despite their dominance and England's propensity to give away penalties, France led by just 14–8 at half time from three penalty goals by Carbonel and a try by Woki to a Smith penalty and an Olowofela try.

French pressure resulted in four further penalty goals by Carbonel, Smith interrupting the flow with three points for England. A close-range drive by replacement prop Joe Heyes and the conversion by fellow bench

man James Grayson gave England hope but, when Carbonel's clever grubber kick laid on a try between the posts for replacement midfielder Adrien Séguret, it was the end for the men in white, a late converted try by Olowofela providing little consolation.

If failure by New Zealand to reach the final had caused gloom back home then you might imagine that defeat in the bronze medal match against South Africa would have triggered a day of national mourning in the South Pacific nation. Yet the Baby Blacks looked to be in charge when they led 25–14 at half time only for South Africa, not for the first time in the tournament, to turn up the heat in the second half, overtaking the title holders for a 42–30 win.

Argentina and Ireland have intruded into the top four in recent seasons but in most years the under-20 semi-finals are made up from a familiar quartet. In age-grade rugby success is dependent on a large base of quality players capable of performing at the exacting levels demanded by these championships. Crucially success is also determined by the number of players in a squad who have experience of Top 14/Pro14/Premiership/Super Rugby/World Sevens.

France had a core of players already hardened by Top 14 rugby while England, for whom skipper Ben Curry, fly half Marcus Smith and wings Gabriel Ibitoye and Jordan Olowofela were outstanding, were not far behind in senior experience.

For countries with smaller resources there will be variability from year to year. In the 2016 championship Ireland reached the final: two years later they were fighting for their lives to avoid relegation and only just survived after defeating Japan 39–33 in a nerve-shredding final round. Scotland, who were fifth in the 2017 championship, were in a similarly perilous position after emerging from the pool stage with no victories, but their win over Ireland in the fourth round removed the threat of dropping to the second-tier Trophy. The Scots then went on to lose to an impressive Georgia side, who, in the 2018 championship, earned all-round respect.

It may be a cliché but the championship is about player development. And that applies irrespective of where a country finishes in the championship. Scotland and Ireland occupied 10th and 11th places respectively but there will be players in both squads who could go on to higher levels of rugby, among them winger Logan Trotter and back row Guy Graham for Scotland, and winger Tom O'Brien and number eight Caelan Doris for Ireland.

Meanwhile the other Celtic nation, Wales, finished in a now familiar 7th position, disappointing perhaps after their opening win over Australia. A heavy defeat to New Zealand may have drained confidence from Wales but they recovered to defeat Japan 18–17 in the final pool match. Wales then lost to Argentina but regrouped

ABOVE Props Demba Bamba (left) and Hassane Kolingar of France celebrate with their team-mates after their 33–25 win in the final.

to defeat Italy in the final round of the tournament. Encouraging for Wales is the fact that twelve of their squad will be eligible for the 2019 edition, among them the talented trio of full back Cai Evans, skipper Tommy Reffell and centre/wing Ryan Conbeer. The future looks bright also for a number of other players in the Welsh squad, notably outside back Ioan Nicholas, fly-half Dan Davies, second row Max Williams and prop Rhys Carre.

For Italy this was another good tournament and proof that their youth programme is moving Italian rugby in a positive direction. Italy finished second in their pool after achieving wins over Scotland and Argentina, earning plaudits for their physical forward play and skill behind the scrum, where fly-half Antonio Rizzi and winger and top try-scorer Giovanni D'Onofrio were hugely impressive.

Elsewhere Australia, with a squad that had Sevens and Super Rugby experience, finished in fifth position while in sixth place were Argentina, who put their poor showing in the 2017 championship firmly behind them. *Los Pumitas* used their traditional forward strength – allied to intelligent back play, much of it borrowed from the sevens game – and posted a powerful performance against Scotland but could not match Italy or England.

There has to be huge sympathy for Japan, who played an exciting style of dynamic and powerful rugby that troubled several of their opponents. The Brave Blossoms lost all their games but the total of Japan's losing margins against Wales, Georgia and Ireland was a mere nine points. But it was enough to relegate Japan, and in 2019 the Brave Blossoms will play in the World Under-20 Trophy.

Meanwhile, after four successive years in the northern hemisphere, the Rugby World Under-20 Championship moves south of the equator for the 2019 edition, to be hosted by Argentina in Rosario and Santa Fe. Expect *Los Pumitas* to put on a strong home show, New Zealand to react to their 2018 'failure' and, who knows, a second successive title for Ntamack and company?

3

SUMMER
TOURS

Back to the Drawing Board?
ENGLAND IN SOUTH AFRICA

by CHRIS JONES

Despite the miserable run, Jones' job was never in genuine danger; he had too much credit in the bank after a near-perfect record for his first two years in the role.

After a poor Six Nations – England's worst performance in 35 years – the South Africa tour took on a new significance. Had the bubble burst on Eddie's England? Or was the run of defeats just a blip on England's path to being the best side in the world? The three-Test series against the Springboks was expected to answer some of those questions.

Jones' squad selection, as usual, was a fascinating one. While there were as many as eight uncapped players (although Cameron Redpath and Jack Willis were unfortunately injured before the tour), it was the inclusion of Danny Cipriani that stole the headlines. For so long one of the form fly halves in the Premiership, Jones had up until now neglected the 30-year-old, with George Ford and Owen Farrell his preferred options at no. 10. But England's Six Nations crash culminated with Jones dropping Ford for the finale against Ireland. Now Cipriani was to get his big chance. Or was he? Would he get an opportunity to run the show against the Boks? Or would he be consigned to bit-part cameos from the replacements bench? The suspicion was that it would be the latter.

Elsewhere, Jones resisted the temptation to rest his British Lions. The likes of Mako Vunipola, Maro Itoje, Jamie George and Owen Farrell – named captain in Dylan Hartley's concussion-enforced absence – all toured. Yes, there were one of two injuries – Ben Te'o the latest big name to withdraw – but the squad nonetheless had an experienced look, with long-term absentees Ben Youngs and Billy Vunipola restored to fitness. The form of the Saracens contingent, who bounced into camp after a resounding Premiership win, didn't hurt either.

The start of the tour was overshadowed by an ongoing row between club and country over Jones' training methods, with the Bath owner Bruce Craig becoming the first high-profile club figure to voice his objections

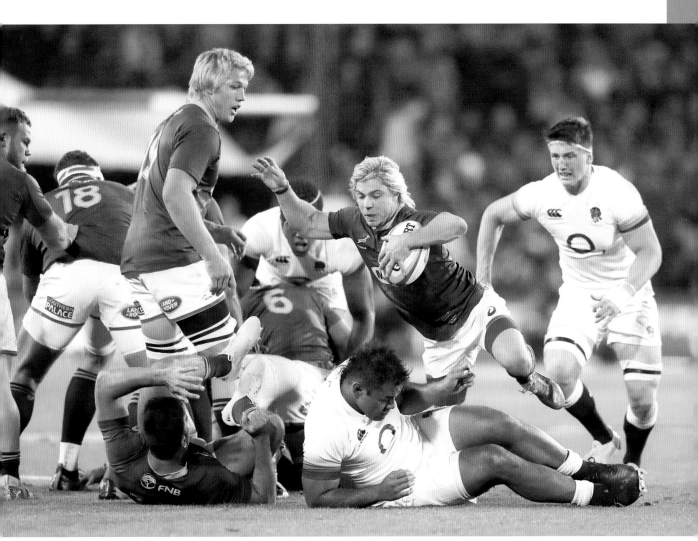

ABOVE Faf de Klerk sets off on a break during the first Test, Ellis Park, 9 June 2018. De Klerk scored South Africa's first try and played an inspirational role in the Springboks' 42–39 win.

LEFT The start England wanted: Mike Brown makes the corner to score the opening try in the first Test.

publicly. Jones returned fire, labelling Craig the 'Donald Trump of rugby' – ironically, this was the nickname once given to Jones himself by Scottish rugby grandee Jim Telfer. But while club and country rows are nothing new, especially in English rugby, it nonetheless heightened the pressure on the England camp, who had taken up residence in the beach town of Umhlaga, just outside Durban, from where they would fly in and out of the Test venues.

Momentous things were happening in South African rugby meanwhile, as new boss Rassie Erasmus made his move. Faf de Klerk and Willie le Roux, outstanding in the Premiership, were recalled from international exile, while Siya Kolisi was named captain. One of the Boks' best players in 2017, Kolisi's appointment made sense from a rugby perspective, but as a black African from a Port Elizabeth township, it means so much more. The Springboks had been led by a black coach in the past, but never by a black captain. Bryan Habana, the great winger, called it an 'unbelievably pivotal moment' in South African history.

Erasmus' team selection also pointed to a new future, with wingers Aphiwe Dyantyi and S'busiso Nkosi making their debuts, along with lock R. G. Snyman, while Lukhanyo Am was winning just a second cap in the centre. The squad had a young and diverse look, as Erasmus looked to balance up his twin objectives as

Springbok coach: transform the racial makeup of the national side, and become the dominant force in the world game. When you throw in the number of top players operating overseas, it's no wonder the South Africa job is considered one of the toughest propositions in rugby coaching.

So, with England in something of a quandary after the Six Nations, and the Springboks embarking on a new era, few knew what to expect when referee Ben O'Keeffe blew his whistle at Ellis Park. What followed was a blitz from the tourists, as England shrugged off the emotionally charged occasion to blow the Boks away with three first-quarter tries. First Mike Brown, out of position on the wing, barged past Handre Pollard to open the scoring, then Jonny May came off his own wing to give Elliot Daly – who had opened the scoring with an absurd penalty from 60 metres – a walk-in. May then roared clear from a brilliant George Ford ball, before laying on the scoring pass to captain Farrell: 24–3, with the Johannesburg crowd in shock.

But back came the Boks. De Klerk had terrorised Premiership defences all season for Sale; now he was doing it on the bigger stage. First he slipped out of Itoje's tackle to score, then he scoured the blindside to put Nkosi clear, with the winger's kick through spilled by Daly. South Africa smelt blood. Le Roux linked with Dyantyi and then Nkosi for a third, before the regal Le Roux glided in for a brilliant fourth after a strong forward surge. The Ellis Park crowd were in raptures, with England reeling.

South Africa picked up where they left off after half-time, with the outstanding Snyman finding Dyantyi shortly after the hour mark. England had no answer to the pace and power, especially at altitude a mile above sea level, with Ellis Park a cauldron of intensity. Eddie Jones had insisted the thin air wouldn't be a factor, but

ABOVE Out of puff? On his debut for England, Brad Shields (left) and back-row colleague Chris Robshaw, during the first Test.

ABOVE RIGHT & RIGHT No smiling faces, whether with Eddie Jones and his team in the coaches' box or with the players on the field at the outcome of the second Test in Bloemfontein.

England looked short of puff, while Jones also declined to use his bench before the final quarter. Itoje touched down with ten minutes to go, but a long-range penalty from Pollard settled matters, even with May's fine last-ditch individual effort.

ABOVE Duane Vermeulen makes a break in the second Test. He scored the Boks' first try as they started to overhaul England's early lead.

RIGHT Centre Lukhanyo Am hunting for an opening during the Bloemfontein Test, eventually won 23–12 by the Springboks.

Jones put on a brave face afterwards, insisting his team could come back from one-nil down in the series. But the questions came thick and fast: why were England training at sea level with the first two Tests at altitude? Why did Jones not use his replacements earlier? Why were they again so ill-disciplined, especially at the breakdown?

Seven days later England were back on the High Veldt, in the modest city of Bloemfontein, with the series on the line. Again, a blistering English start: Billy Vunipola with the bust, Ford, Farrell, May with the hands – and Brown strolling over. Then Brown, always in the game, made space for May, who finished superbly. But England were unable to keep the foot on the Springbok throat, with Tendai Mtawarira – on his 100th appearance for his country – storming into the 22, and Duane Vermeulen bulldozing over from 20 metres. Pollard kicked a monster penalty and the Boks led by a point at the break.

England had nothing after half-time. A spell of scrum pressure resulted in a Springbok penalty try, and with Jones again reluctant to use his bench, South Africa made the game safe with another Pollard goal. It felt like déjà-vu for the tourists, as defeat became a familiar tale. Five Test losses in a row now, and the series gone.

Back in 2016, Jones had run rings around his opposite number Michael Cheika on and off the field as his side walloped the Wallabies 3–0, but, two years on, the England boss seemed to have lost his magic touch. England went back to Durban with their wounds raw and the vultures circling.

Despite the miserable run, Jones' job was never in genuine danger; he had too much credit in the bank after a near-perfect record for his first two years in the role. But both media and fans alike were entitled to search for answers, especially with the World Cup in Japan edging ever closer. Jones' regime had always been about winning: the controversial selections (Brad Shields, for example, had walked into an England Test jersey just days after arriving in camp), the no-expense-spared training centres, the tensions with the clubs – all things that were excused in the midst of a victorious streak, but less so with the defeats coming thick and fast.

Although the series was lost, England had to win in Cape Town to stop the rot, especially with a dangerous autumn series on the way featuring South Africa again, Australia, and the mighty All Blacks. Once more Jones went conservative with his selection, bringing back Chris Robshaw for the unwell Shields, sticking with Youngs at scrum-half, and replacing the unavailable Vunipolas with the experienced Joe Marler and Nathan Hughes. The England boss did, however, make a significant change at fly-half, with Cipriani getting a treasured opportunity in place of Ford – incredibly, it was Cipriani's first start in ten years.

In reality, Cipriani struggled to get into the game in filthy conditions at Newlands, but produced an inspired intervention with ten minutes to go to seal a priceless win. His under-pressure cross-kick found a sprinting Jonny May, who scored his third try of the series to cap a magnificent few weeks for the Leicester flyer. Farrell's boot did the rest, with 20 points from the nerveless England skipper, as the senior players stood up to salvage something from the summer.

Jones stressed afterwards his team would be much better for the series defeat and the poor run of form. But as his players – and the head coach himself – headed to the beach for a much-needed break, the questions being asked before the tour still remained.

Youngsters Make Their Mark
WALES IN THE AMERICAS

by **HUGH GODWIN**

Warren Gatland's verdict was delivered with a broad smile: 'The boys have been brilliant on and off the field, and we've achieved all the things we wanted to do. It's great for Welsh rugby.'

Warren Gatland's verdict on Wales's three-match summer tour to the Americas was delivered with a broad smile on his grey-whiskered face. 'This whole experience was about giving players opportunities,' the head coach said. 'The boys have been brilliant on and off the field, and we've achieved all the things we wanted to do. It's great for Welsh rugby.'

It was stretching a point for the first leg of the trip to be accorded the status of a full Test, as a Welsh team lacking maybe 20 first-choice players edged out a mostly third- and fourth-string South Africa by 22 points to 20 in neutral Washington, DC. But attitudes hardened when Wales travelled 5,000 miles south to face Argentina twice in the Pumas' own lair. They strengthened the line-up a little while still experimenting, so a clean sweep with wide winning margins was an undeniably impressive result.

The Wales players visited the Abraham Lincoln memorial before their country's fifth Test on US soil and a line from the old president might have been an apt slogan: 'The best way to predict your future is to create it.' Gatland had chosen to rest most of Wales's British & Irish Lions from 2017, including such stalwarts as Alun Wyn Jones, Taulupe Faletau, Justin Tipuric, Dan Biggar, Liam Williams, Leigh Halfpenny and Ken Owens. Those absent injured included Jonathan Davies, Sam Warburton, Jake Ball, Aaron Shingler, Dan Lydiate, Josh Navidi, Scott Baldwin, Rory Thornton and Tyler Morgan. And there was also the baffling tale of the 'Premiership Three' – the English-based players Josh Adams, Tom Francis and Luke Charteris who were named in the squad then dropped to comply with English Premiership regulations, before Adams and Francis were called to Argentina, after all.

Gatland designated the Cardiff Blues forwards Cory Hill and Ellis Jenkins as tour co-captains, and they had their regional club-mates Tomos Williams and Gareth Anscombe as the half-backs for the opening match, with Jenkins, playing only his seventh Test, as the on-field skipper. George North started at centre for the fourth time in his 74 Wales Tests, and the front row of Nicky Smith, Elliot Dee and Dillon Lewis had nine caps between them. Most of the available Scarlets were rested, a week after their Pro14 final.

South Africa's first Test under new coach Rassie Erasmus featured seven Test debutants from the start and another six on the bench. Only Pieter-Steph du Toit, Wilco Louw and Chiliboy Ralepele from the run-on pack in Washington would go on to see action in the subsequent home series against England, and the starting midfield of Elton Jantjies, the highly physical André Esterhuizen and Jesse Kriel was only picked together again for the dead-rubber third Test with the English in Cape Town.

At Washington's RFK Memorial Stadium, a turnover penalty inside the first 20 seconds set the tone for a bitty, stop-start match of reset scrums and scrappy handling. Wales sought a high tempo but incessant drizzle and freshly minted combinations undermined these high ideals. South Africa favoured the driving maul and midfield bashing by Esterhuizen.

It was the stocky, obdurately effervescent Jenkins who rose most obviously above the mediocrity and the open-side flanker made a typical pilfer after the tackle to snuff out a rare Springbok visit to the Wales 22 and keep his side 14–3 ahead going into half-time. Jenkins also closed the match out with a similar intervention, burrowing under a pod of three South African forwards.

Wales had taken the lead in the 31st minute, in response to a penalty by Jantjies, as Anscombe launched a high ball, Owen Watkin gave chase and Jenkins pickpocketed Bok full-back Curwin Bosch behind a ruck. Quick

ABOVE Springbok winger Travis Ismaiel tries to find a way past Gareth Anscombe (10) and Hadleigh Parkes (23) during the match at RFK Stadium in Washington, DC, on 2 June 2018.

hands put Hallam Amos over for a try, to be followed three minutes later by Tomos Williams scrambling determinedly over from a ruck near the goal-line. Both tries were converted by Anscombe.

An interception by right wing Travis Ismaiel gave the Boks a try three minutes into the second half, Anscombe kicked a penalty for Wales, then Watkin went to the sin bin and South Africa immediately drove off a couple of scrums to make a try for left wing Makazole Mapimpi. A scrum penalty conceded by Wales on their 22-metre line allowed replacement Robert du Preez a simple kick and South Africa led 20–17 with seven minutes remaining.

Du Preez motioned for his team-mates to stay calm, but he was anything but as the Boks made trouble for themselves with a pass into their 22, and poor Du Preez was charged down by Williams twice in very quick succession; the second of them, in the in-goal area, ricocheted off the unlucky Ismaiel towards Ryan Elias and the 23-year-old replacement hooker had only to flop on the ball to score.

Pausing only to mark centre Hadleigh Parkes' post-tour nuptials with a modest stag party in Washington, the Welsh flew to Argentina, to find a Pumas team based squarely on the Jaguares side who had just posted a sixth straight win in Super Rugby. The Welsh retained Amos at full-back and North reverted to the wing, while up front Rob Evans was restored at loosehead prop, and Hill, Seb Davies and number eight Ross Moriarty were augmented by the incoming Adam Beard and James Davies, with Jenkins omitted on rotation. Hill skippered the team in Argentina, but it would a huge surprise if Jenkins' day does not come again.

On a good playing surface in the western desert near the Andes, the Welsh had a mountainous lead of 17–3 by half-time. Patchell's penalty followed his conversions of tries by James Davies – in at the corner from a neat

offload by Amos – and North, who combined with returning scrum-half Gareth Davies to punch through a Pumas line-out. This elevated North to third place on the all-time Wales try-scorer list, with 34 to the 58 by the record-holder Shane Williams, and 40 by Gareth Thomas.

As Parkes resumed the tidy playmaking that was his hallmark in the Six Nations Championship, Wales smashed Argentina's heavier runners before they could reach the gain line. Sharp work at the breakdown, kicks to keep the ball in play and quickly tapped free-kicks all forced the Pumas to build attacks from perilously deep positions. The Welsh cause was further boosted by Evans'

brilliant hold-up tackle on the line, while Pumas fly-half Nicolás Sánchez kicked one attacking penalty touch-finder dead and his team chose to turn down several shots at the posts.

Remarkably it took until the 78th minute for Argentina to find a try, through replacement back-rower Tomás Lezana. Then Santiago González Iglesias was whistled for holding on in his 22, and Anscombe, on from the bench, added a penalty to one kicked by Patchell earlier in the half, to complete a win by 23 points to 10.

'We defended sensationally well and it's a while since I've seen a group of players this hungry,' said an approving Gatland.

For the second Test in Sante Fe, Wales brought Watkin and Aled Davies in for Parkes and Gareth Davies, while Elias and Tom Francis were drafted into the front row and Jenkins wore the no. 6 jersey ahead of Seb Davies. The Argentina coach Daniel Hourcade chose only to swap the 80-times-capped Martín Landajo in for Gonzalo Bertanou at scrum half.

But the pattern of the match was similar, with Wales again firmly in control, and 19–5 up at the interval. Argentina made seven handing errors to their opponents' one before home wing Bautista Delguy nabbed a try

Eastdil Secured

is proud to support

Wooden Spoon Rugby World

ABOVE Second row opponents. Cory Hill breaks free from Matías Alemanno's attempted tackle late in the second Test.

just before half-time. Adams had scored the individual try of the tour in the 23rd minute, turning on his heel to scoop a loose ball up near the halfway line before he burst through a thicket of Argentina players with a sidestep off his right foot and another off his left. It was a first Test try on his fourth appearance by the Swansea-born Worcester Warrior.

Patchell's conversion and four penalty goals made up the rest of the first-half scoring, and Wales went on to add another two penalties from the fly-half plus a lovely team try with 55 minutes gone. It stemmed from aggressive defence. Jerónimo de la Fuente's grubber rebounded over the centre's head, and North and Parkes' midfield partner Scott Williams harried the resulting breakdown. Landajo had a box-kick partially charged down by Beard, which led to a kick into the Argentina 22 by Amos and a grounding for a drop-out that gave Wales possession. Whereupon snappy, accurate passes by Patchell, Scott Williams, Amos and Moriarty sent North sprinting down the left touchline, and he made one final perfect delivery to the scorer, Amos.

At 30–5, and with regulation time up, it was a shame Moriarty, who had played so well on tour, lost his temper in a spat with Nicolás Sánchez and grabbed the Puma fly half round the neck. A medic from the Argentina staff angrily pushed the Welshman's mouth away from Sanchez's head. Moriarty was sent off by referee Jaco Peyper and received a suspension of four weeks.

There was enough time left for replacement hooker Julián Montoya to score a try for Argentina but all the plaudits went to Wales, winners by 30–12. 'The group has worked particularly hard and it's nice to know hard work does get rewarded,' said Patchell, who kicked 30 points in his two matches. Gatland added: 'There are probably a few older guys sitting at home, a little worried at the moment.'

The truth of that statement will be seen in due course although Wales will surely be leaving several proven back-rowers and a couple of fine scrum halves out when they select for the 2019 World Cup. As for Argentina, who had Scotland still to play (and a bigger loss in store), this series marked the beginning of the end for Hourcade, who resigned after five years in the job.

Hard-fought Series Win
IRELAND IN AUSTRALIA

by **PETER O'REILLY**

A year from the World Cup, Ireland look in good order. It's true, they play an attritional, asphyxiating style, and none of the top-tier nations work quite so hard for their points. But what must they be like to play against?

A taut, tense Test series concluded, appropriately enough, with a scene of high suspense at Sydney's Allianz Stadium, well after the hooter had sounded. With Ireland leading 20–16, all 46 players, two coaching teams and a crowd of over 44,000 were on tenterhooks as they awaited the outcome of a conversation between referee Pascal Gaüzère and his TMO, Ben Skeen.

After 240 minutes of high-class rugby over the course of three weekends, it would all come down to Skeen's judgement. Had Bernard Foley's pass been deflected by Jacob Stockdale's flailing arm? Had a potential try been illegally prevented?

On the giant screens at either end of the stadium, the flight of the ball was tracked in super slow-mo from a variety of angles until finally a judgement was delivered, audible initially only to TV viewers and the two players closest to the referee – acting captains Johnny Sexton and David Pocock.

'Pascal,' Skeen said, 'I must have clear and obvious evidence.' Sexton leaned closer to hear the killer line, then clenched his fist in celebration. 'There is no clear evidence the green player touched the ball.' Victory for Ireland.

In truth, no one really wants such an entertaining series to be decided in this way. But it does say something about the nature of the rivalry between the two teams, whose aggregate scores over the course of three Tests were level at 55–55. This is surely the sort of tussle the SANZAR nations had in mind when they bartered their European counterparts for a best-of-three format for the June Test window. A three-game series would be easier to market, they argued, because it carried the possibility of a 'final', a deciding Test match.

It turns out that between Wales, France, England and Ireland, there have been 13 South v. North series in the past seven years but only two of those have gone down to the wire: Ireland in South Africa in 2016, when they lost the decider in Port Elizabeth, and now Ireland in Australia 2018. No wonder that the Aussies were so pleased that Ireland are due to visit again in 2020.

The tourists brought huge numbers of supporters, especially for the Melbourne and Sydney tests, and of course they confirmed their status as the pre-eminent side in Europe, as genuine contenders for the Rugby World Cup in Japan.

Johnny Sexton, their talisman and their director-in-chief, has already said one of Ireland's role models is the England side of 2003, for whom winning a series in the Southern Hemisphere – in their case New Zealand in 2002 – was a major building block on the way towards becoming the only European team to win the Webb Ellis Trophy.

There was another historical motivation here – the knowledge that Ireland hadn't won a Test match, or a Test series in Australia since Ollie Campbell steered them to victory in 1979, all of 39 years previously – in other words, before any of this squad were born. Ten Tests, ten defeats.

For all that, they had to deal with massive expectations on this venture – and Irish teams don't tend to feel comfortable in this situation. Winning the Grand Slam meant that they travelled as 'comfortable' favourites, all the more so as they were close to full strength. Skipper Rory Best had to withdraw with a hamstring pull and three flankers – Sean O'Brien, Rhys Ruddock and Josh

RIGHT Rob Kearney can't quite complete his aerial challenge with winger Dane Haylett-Petty during the decisive third Test.

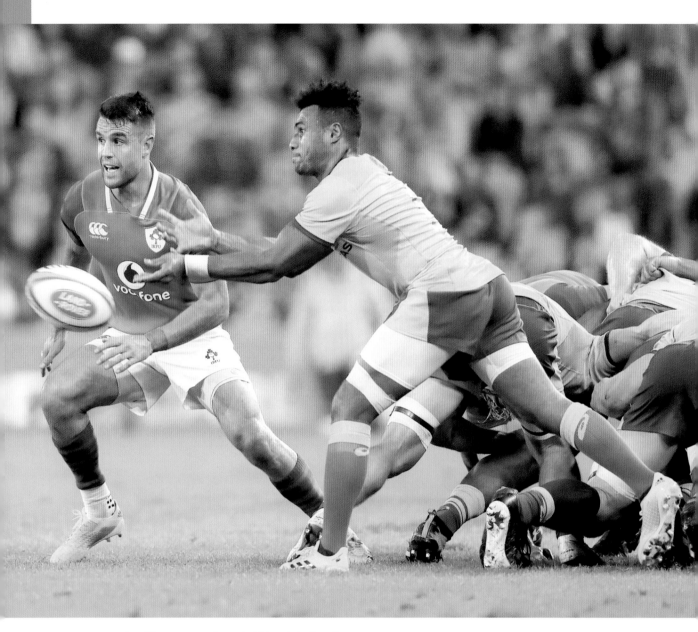

van der Flier – were also rehabbing injuries. Everyone else was fit and keen to travel.

The Wallabies, meanwhile, had won only seven of 14 Tests in 2017. Their most recent outing, in Edinburgh the previous November, had resulted in an embarrassing 24–53 defeat. Australia's Super Rugby sides had been struggling, too, especially against New Zealand opposition. Their administrators were under constant attack in the media for their supposed failure to mind the grass roots of their sport.

ABOVE Two of the finest scrum halves in world rugby: Conor Murray watches Will Genia get his pass away during Australia's 18–9 first-Test win. Genia took the man of the match award.

LEFT Centre partners Robbie Henshaw and Bundee Aki tackle Kurtley Beale during the fiercely contested third Test.

Naturally Ireland coach Joe Schmidt tried to talk the Wallabies up, stressing that they'd beaten the All Blacks in their last Test at Brisbane's Suncorp Stadium, where the first Test would be played. He mentioned the return of David Pocock from the player's self-imposed 18-month exile from Test rugby – and sure enough, the flanker was to play a hugely influential role in the series.

But people were less inclined to take Schmidt seriously when he rolled the dice with selection for the first game, resting Sexton along with his first-choice props Cian Healy and Tadhg Furlong. The coach explained that he needed to give fringe players experience at the highest level, to cover himself for injuries at the World Cup. Hence Joey Carbery was given only his third start at fly-half of the season, for any team, while John Ryan and Rob Herring were given a run in the front row.

All three performed credibly enough at Suncorp – but Ireland lost 18–9. The irony was that when Sexton led the cavalry off the bench in the third quarter, Ireland led 9–8, having survived a ropy period at the end of the first half, when Foley, the Wallabies' fly half, scored in the left corner. Disconcertingly for the tourists, they stuttered badly on the homeward stretch. Sexton and Conor Murray made errors at key moments. Uncharacteristically, Murray lost his cool with referee Marius van der Westhuizen.

The scrum crumpled under pressure, allowing Foley to kick the Wallabies in front. Suitably emboldened, skipper Michael Hooper opted to run the next penalty that came their way and had his reward when Pocock crashed over from short range. 1–0 to the Wallabies.

The temperature was a good few degrees cooler down in Melbourne, and the mood in Ireland's team hotel was verging on frosty. As defence coach Andy Farrell pointed out, the tourists had come second in areas of the game where they tended to dominate: in the contact zones, where Pocock and Hooper had edged things, and especially in the aerial battle, where Israel Folau had been supreme.

Most strikingly of all, Farrell appeared to question Ireland's desire in comparison to that of the Australians and did so in public: 'We'll see what the good old-fashioned Irish ticker's about, won't we?' he said. When the tour was over, a couple of players would describe this as a turning point.

Schmidt selected his strongest available side for the second Test, with the only surprise being at hooker, where Niall Scannell was chosen to start – evidently, that scrum penalty towards the end of the first Test had been pinned at least partially on Sean Cronin.

Ireland started disastrously, conceding a try to Kurtley Beale inside 90 seconds, but responded impressively. They cashed in fully on a yellow card by Marika Koroibete for a tip tackle on Rob Kearney, registering 13 points in his absence. The Aussies' indiscipline was a theme for the series but Ireland's penalty count was high as well. Cian Healy was binned for collapsing a maul and despite dominating possession, Ireland only led 16–14 at the break.

True to their Six Nations form, they started the second half strongly, with Furlong capping a fine all-round performance with his first international try. A late rally by the Wallabies gave the tourists a scare but their defence held out and the series was squared.

To Sydney – but not before a few whinges from Wallabies coach Michael Cheika, who complained – unjustifiably, as it turned out – that Will Genia's broken forearm had been the result of foul play, and that Folau had been 'blocked' from challenging in the air. It was all heating up nicely.

The first half in Sydney brought no tries but was not without incident. Both skippers, Peter O'Mahony and Michael Hooper, departed through injury. That O'Mahony was stretchered off probably had something to do with Folau being carded for what Skeen saw as an illegal aerial challenge. One of many hotly debated decisions.

Ireland led 12–9 at the break and never relinquished that lead. They scored early in the third quarter again, with man of the match CJ Stander being driven over off a line-out maul. From there, however, they were under severe pressure at the scrum and out wide, as the Wallabies went up several gears. Ireland's defence was tremendous, though, containing their opponents to one Koroibete try, and holding out for a 16–10 win through that incredibly tense end-game.

Ireland's composure, epitomised by the way Sexton retained control despite being on the end of some bone-shaking hits, was ultimately the difference between the sides. As for Joe Schmidt, he achieved his twin objectives. He won the series and simultaneously gave valuable experience to fringe players. Scannell and Herring look viable alternatives to Best, Jack Conan made the most of his opportunity at number eight in Sydney. Meanwhile Jordan Larmour was asked to fill in for Kearney when the heat was on in that final quarter, and never put a foot wrong.

A year out from the World Cup, Ireland look in good order. It's true, they play an attritional, asphyxiating style, and none of the top-tier nations work quite so hard for their points. But what must they be like to play against?

It's true also that they rely too heavily on Sexton and Murray, with the scrum half spending all but two minutes of the Test series on the pitch. But which top side does not have its indispensables? Besides, it should be easier to manage players through at this World Cup, given the pool games get progressively easier, in theory: Scotland, Japan, Russia and Samoa.

What's more, this series was the best possible preparation for the knock-out stages – three tight, high-quality Tests in three weeks. Ireland have never made it to the last four but on recent evidence, they are ready to make more history.

ABOVE Flanker Dan Leavy and full back Israel Folau contest a high ball during the second Test, won 26–21 by Ireland.

LEFT Tadhg Furlong is just caught by second row Izack Rodda during the third Test. Furlong was impressive with ball in hand throughout the series, with a try in the second Test.

Testing Younger Players
SCOTLAND IN THE AMERICAS

by **ALAN LORIMER**

At the end of three weeks on tour several members of the squad had, as near as possible, written their names on the passenger list for Japan . . . Scotland's prospects suddenly look a whole lot better.

If Scotland's 2018 rugby tourists had 'wanted to be in America' then their wish was realised in spades with an itinerary that embraced Canada, USA and Argentina, mirroring the trail set by Vern Cotter's squad four years earlier in 2014. The hope was that the 2018 squad could emulate their predecessors but, while results were important, head coach Gregor Townsend's real focus was on the make-up of his 2019 World Cup squad

Having left a number of senior players back home, Townsend wanted to run the rule over the next in line. And at the end of three weeks on tour several members of the squad had, as near as possible, written their names on the passenger list for Japan.

The first round of 'Scotland's Got Talent' was hosted by the city of Edmonton, where the Scots faced Canada, then ranked 21st in World Rugby, modest enough for Townsend to risk selecting four uncapped players in his match-day squad.

In the event the Scotland head coach was repaid with encouraging performances from all four debutants, and especially from benchmen Adam Hastings (son of Gavin) at fly half and Lewis Carmichael in the second row. The other two first cappers, Harlequins centre James Lang, and the Edinburgh flanker Jamie Ritchie, both named in the starting team, also merited their first international honour.

The quartet of newcomers, however, might have wanted a sterner examination than Canada offered. The Canucks, while competitive in world sevens, have taken a step back in XVs rugby, as was evident by their bluntness in attack, albeit partially compensated for by a doughty defence.

Nor ultimately was Canada's forward strength able to cope with the Scots' pack, who, in wet conditions, focused on mauling, indirectly leading to a first-half score by fly half Ruaridh Jackson and directly to a second-half hat-trick from hooker George Turner. The Scots' other tries in their 48–10 win came from wing Byron McGuigan, flanker Magnus Bradbury and replacement Carmichael.

If Canada had provided the Scots with an easy opening tour match then the game in a climatically challenging Houston, Texas, against the USA was to deliver the shock therapy that Townsend's players perhaps needed.

USA, as is clear from their World Series results, have performed well in international sevens, but their XVs game, too, is on an upward trajectory, in no small part due to the setting up of a professional league and to the inspiring coaching of Gary Gold. Before facing Scotland, the Eagles had won all six of their international matches in 2018 and a week before taking on the Scots they had defeated World Cup qualifiers Russia 62–13.

Townsend was perfectly aware of the USA threat but, even so, he named two uncapped players, scrum half George Horne and back row Matt Fagerson, playing alongside their brothers Pete Horne and Zander Fagerson, in a relatively inexperienced side, skippered for the first time by Stuart Hogg.

Scotland's blistering start put the tourists ahead 7–0 after barely two minutes from Kinghorn's converted try, carved out by Hogg. A penalty try resulting from quick interplay between the Horne brothers and then a line-out maul try from Turner, converted by Kinghorn, gave the Scots a 21–3 advantage.

With such a tidy lead what could possibly go wrong for Scotland? A lot as it happened. USA's heavier and more physical forwards were increasingly dominating key areas and moreover their muscular centres, Paul Lasike and Bryce Campbell along with wing Blaine Scully, were causing problems both in attack and defence. The net result was a second penalty goal by the impressive Sale fly half, A. J. McGinty, and his conversion of a

ABOVE (From left) Simon Berghan, Magnus Bradbury and Ben Toolis lead a powerful Scotland forward drive for the Canada line.

try by the former Worcester hooker, Joe Taufete'e. Scotland, however, regained some ground with a Kinghorn penalty for a 24–13 half time lead.

Then in the third quarter, the match unravelled further for Scotland as the under-pressure tourists conceded a string of penalties. Taufete'e smashed his way over for his second try from a line-out maul, McGinty converted and the fly half then added a third penalty goal to bring his side within a point of the Scots.

With the game finely balanced debutant Matt Fagerson spilled a high ball from McGinty, and when the Eagles' fly half gathered on the follow-up, flanker Hanco Germishuys was on hand to take the scoring pass for a try in the corner. McGinty added what ultimately proved to be the winning conversion points for a 30–24 lead.

Townsend brought on experience from the bench and Scotland rallied in the final ten minutes, eventually scoring in stoppage time when fly-half Hastings' long pass allowed fellow replacement Dougie Fife to score wide out. Kinghorn, however, missed the touchline conversion, leaving the USA to celebrate a 30–29 victory. It was the first time the Eagles had achieved a win against a Tier 1 side in the modern era and perhaps was a turning point for the sport in USA.

'We gave them momentum in that third quarter through ill-discipline,' Townsend conceded after the defeat, adding: 'A couple of penalties gave them field position. They had a lot of possession and got a try through an error – which happens especially when the ball is slippery.'

Scotland, by fielding a less than strong team, had paid the price for not respecting the USA's recent Test-match record, but the dividend was a number of youngsters, notably half backs Horne and Hastings, being exposed to tough Test conditions.

For the third tour match against Argentina in Resistencia, Townsend, who had reduced his squad by five, opted to keep the half-back pairing of Horne and Hastings and, in fact, made only one change to the backline, bringing in Dougie Fife to the starting team.

But in the forward pack seven changes were made. Townsend, knowing that he would need more experienced forwards to face Argentina, reverted to props Alan Dell and Simon Berghan and selected, for the first time on the tour, skipper and hooker, Stuart McInally, who had missed the first two matches because of a calf injury.

The back row, too, was recast with the return of Magnus Bradbury and David Denton to supply genuine 'grunt' together with the eyebrow-raising selection of Fraser Brown, normally a hooker, on the open-side flank. The other change was Grant Gilchrist resuming at second row.

Scotland needed a restoration of confidence after the USA set-back: the performance against Argentina, which produced a 44–15 win for the Scots, supplied it in bucketloads. Admittedly Argentina, on the back of successive defeats to Wales on the previous two weekends, and about to part company with their head coach,

ABOVE Flanker Magnus Bradbury grapples unsuccessfully for the ball in a maul, Argentina *v*. Scotland, 23 June 2018.

LEFT Scotland winger Blair Kinghorn breaks through the USA Eagles cover, beating the tackle of scrum half Shaun Davies (left). Bradbury and Kinghorn both enhanced their reputations on tour.

Daniel Hourcade, seemed out of sorts, lacking the forward aggression and back-play panache that in the past has troubled touring teams.

Townsend has always been a proponent of dynamic rugby and against Argentina his charges played with such quick tempo that they led 36–3 at half time from breathtaking tries by George Horne (2), Kinghorn, McInally and Bradbury, and the goal-kicking of Pete Horne.

Heavy rain after half-time made handling more difficult and put a brake on the Scots' scoring machine. In fact it was Argentina who struck first in the second period with a try by Tomas Lezana from a line-out ricochet, Nicolás Sánchez adding to his earlier penalty goal with the conversion.

But any notion of a Puma fightback was quickly nipped in the bud when Dougie Fife scored in the corner from Hogg's long pass, putting a Scotland victory beyond doubt. Argentina to their credit conjured a late try for Santiago Iglesias, but Scotland replied with a Horne penalty to give Scotland their biggest away win over the Pumas.

What was pleasing for Townsend was the way his side produced the style of rugby that matches his vision. The forwards were accurate and powerful at the breakdown allowing the pacy combination of Horne and Hastings to outplay their more experienced Puma opponents.

Horne's outstanding display against the Pumas will surely put him high up in the queue for the no. 9 jersey while at fly half Hastings looks to be the answer as back-up to Finn Russell. Elsewhere in the backs, Kinghorn added to his growing reputation, Lang is likely to be given further opportunities, Fife made his case for a return to the international team and Pete Horne reaffirmed his value as an inside centre.

Among the forwards McInally, used his one opportunity to restate his qualities as both a player and a leader, Turner continued a remarkable year with strong displays at hooker, Berghan and Dell edged ahead in the props department, Gilchrist and Ben Toolis impressed in the second row, while in the back row Magnus Bradbury and David Denton could provide Scotland with the ball-carrying strength missing in the Scotland team's make-up.

One disappointment for Townsend was not being able to assess Duncan Taylor, the Saracens utility back having failed to recover from the back injury that kept him out of action for much of last season.

Overall, and despite the (narrow) defeat to USA – another reminder of the Scots' inconsistency – the tour was a success. It proved that despite having small playing-numbers, Scotland's strength in depth is less shallow than is sometimes feared. Moreover the tour showed that Townsend is proving to be an astute coach, who knows both how to spot and how to harness talent. Scotland's prospects for Japan suddenly look a whole lot better and as for their tour vanquishers: 'everything's fine in America'.

BELOW Scotland fly half Adam Hastings breaks through to set up George Horne for an early try.

4

HOME
FRONT

Living up to Early Promise
THE NEXT GENERATION

by CHRIS JONES

All too often a log-jam at Premiership level has stopped the best young players from gaining vital first-team experience. Now there appears to be a concerted effort by the clubs to give youth its head.

It is a measure of how young talent is being fast-tracked into Eddie Jones's squad that while Ben Curry was leading England in their U20 World Cup final against France, his twin brother Tom was playing open-side flanker for the senior team in their three-Test series with South Africa.

With the World Cup in Japan next year fast approaching, players with barely a couple of seasons in the Premiership are putting forward genuine cases for inclusion in the England squad.

RIGHT Brothers under pressure. Tom Curry gets set to attack a South African ball-carrier, first Test, 9 June 2018, Johannesburg, South Africa. Brother Ben (below right) faces different demands, meeting the media as England captain before the World U20 Championship final.

BELOW LEFT Ben Earl of Saracens makes a break during the Aviva Premiership match between Saracens and Bath Rugby at Allianz Park on 15 April 2018. Saracens won 41–6.

Tom Curry, of Sale, performed so well against the Springboks that he is now the obvious no. 7 for the autumn Tests, which include a clash with New Zealand at Twickenham on November. That is when Curry and the rest of the England young guns who get into the match 23 will discover just what playing the best team on the planet involves.

The All Blacks are constantly drip-feeding new talent into their ranks and, at last, England are doing the same. The Saracens pair of Ben Earl and Nick Isiekwe, who like Tom Curry were in South Africa, were also still qualified to take part in the U20 World Cup that France won. In the squad beaten by the French was Harlequins outside half Marcus Smith and James Grayson, son of former England World Cup winner Paul.

The England U20 set-up has been delivering high-quality talent for years but there has all too often been a log-jam at Premiership level that has stopped the best from gaining vital first-team experience. Now, there appears to be a concerted effort by the clubs to give youth its head with Jim Mallinder's son Harry making a real impact at Northampton.

Jim may have gone but Harry remains a key figure in their squad and, just like Bath number eight Zach Mercer, has already caught the eye of Jones, who shocked many in the game by plucking 18-year-old Cameron Redpath out of Sedbergh School, which produced fellow centres Will Carling and Will Greenwood, and naming him in the tour squad for South Africa. It was a move guaranteed to grab headlines as the Sale academy player was not only largely unknown in the game, but he is also the son of former Scotland captain Bryan!

Unfortunately, Cameron suffered the same fate as 20-year-old Wasps flanker Jack Willis and pulled out of the tour to have knee surgery, which means his dad, now the Scotland U20 coach, could yet convince his son to opt for the dark blue of Scotland rather than the white shirt with the red rose.

Knowing when a young player is ready to make the switch from age-group representative rugby to the professional game is always difficult, although when you are Isiekwe and 6 ft 7 in and 18 st, then the transition is rather easier! For Smith at Harlequins, last season was supposed to be a slow burner as he had just finished his A levels at Brighton College and needed time to bed in to the club where All Black Nick Evans had retired from the no. 10 role and become attack coach. Then Demetri Catrakilis and Tim Swiel, the more experienced outside-half options, both got injured forcing John Kingston, then director of rugby, to hand the starting role to his young gun.

It was a massive challenge for Smith, who experienced understandable highs and lows in his first season, one that saw him make 28 appearances and score an impressive 199 points, including three tries. For Smith the challenge in his vital second season will be to learn from his mistakes, recognise that defences will now be aware of what he likes to do in attack and come up with new 'tricks' to ensure he remains a genuine contender for an England squad place.

The Quins end of season awards saw him pick up the Players' Player of the Season, Supporters' Player of the Season and Young Player of the Season awards. The outside half was also nominated for BBC Young Sports Personality of the Year and won the Young Sportsman of the Year at the British Ethnic Diversity Sports Awards (BEDSA) to give you an idea of the impact he made and what he has to live up to when it all starts again in September.

Kingston said: 'Marcus is an intelligent and humble young lad who is very focused on his rugby. He has the talent and abilities to take this Quins side forward to the next stage of its development. He is the type of player and person that perfectly embodies the Harlequins spirit and culture at The Stoop.'

Jones is equally convinced that Smith has the right stuff, although he is quick to tell the teenager that he has to run straighter rather than moving sideways with ball in hand to evade the defence. Jones said: 'We want to develop him as a player. I see him as an important investment for English rugby. We'd ideally like to get him right for the World Cup because then he fills a role as a third stand-off for us. The only way we're going to develop him is to allow him to play for Harlequins and then bring him into camps and try and put extra work into him.'

Jones is right to highlight the opportunities that a young player must get to gain the experience that convinces the doubters they have the capacity to move up the selection gears without spending too long in neutral.

RIGHT Nick Isiekwe of Saracens puts in a last-ditch try-saving tackle on Kahn Fotuali'i of Bath.

BELOW RIGHT Marcus Smith of Harlequins breaks away to score for Harlequins *v.* Exeter 5 May 2018.

BELOW Cameron Redpath of Sale Sharks holds off Saracens tacklers during an Anglo-Welsh Cup match in November 2017.

Getting obsessed about a player's age is something Kingston did not believe was relevant when looking at Smith and explained: 'This is not some sort of gimmick because he's young – I don't give a rats how old he is, I give a rats about what he's able to do. When you have guys coming in at 18, and we've had a lot over the years, you've got to be looking at what his physical condition is like, in terms of how they are and how advanced they are.

'Not all of the [young players] will be at the same level as your seasoned professional who has had who knows how many seasons, they're not going to be at that level so it's just lunacy not to work with people, like Marcus, to assess how much rugby they need, when they will step in and out; he will jump at every opportunity he gets.'

The reason players like the Curry twins, Isiekwe, Earl and Smith are able to thrive in a fiercely physical sport is thanks to the work of the club academies which prepare them for the demands of professional rugby, both physically and mentally. Injuries happen to players of all ages and just because you are new to the game does not mean you are bound to spend months on the treatment table thanks to the heavier hits that are put in at the highest level of the sport

Isiekwe is just a likely to make an opponent wince as feel the same kind of effect of a big impact because of his natural size and the carefully controlled conditioning regime that is provided at Saracens. The expertise of the Premiership academy coaches and staff is the reason why the Curry twins are making a big impact and why Smith has managed to gain so much vital experience of outside-half play in arguably the toughest club competition in world rugby. For 20-year-old powerhouse wing Joe Cokanasiga staying in the top flight to showcase your talent is vital and that is why he quit relegated London Irish to join Mercer at Bath and remain in Jones's thoughts.

Now, all these youngster have to do is repeat it all over again while dealing with a massive weight of expectation. Welcome to the big time!

BELOW London Irish's Joe Cokanasiga in action during the Aviva Premiership match with Bath Rugby, 5 May 2018, in Bath.

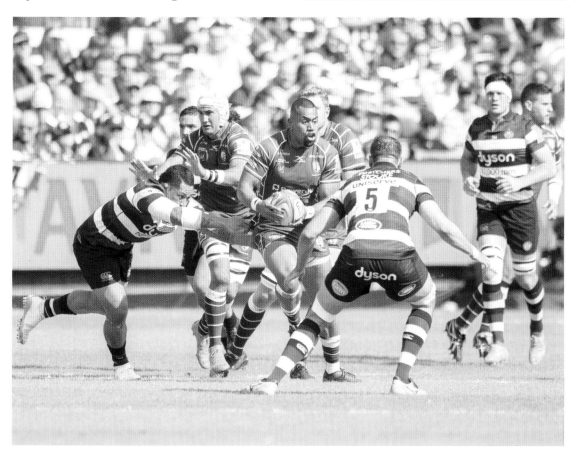

Back from Death's Door
THE RE-BIRTH OF COVENTRY

by **NEALE HARVEY**

'There are no limits to what this club can achieve. We're in a fantastic location and there's a lot of goodwill towards us now – all we have to do is to ensure that we put the right plans in place to fulfil our potential.'

Friday 13 June 2008 is a day nobody at Coventry Rugby will ever forget. Years of financial decay had left a once proud club at death's door and, barring the lodging of a £100,000 bond, the Rugby Football Union had been ready to pull the plug and send the club hurtling into oblivion.

As the hours to a 3.30 p.m. deadline ticked by it became apparent that the cash would not be forthcoming and it seemed to be game over. However, the intervention of former *Coventry Telegraph* sports reporter John Wilkinson proved crucial as an exchange of emails and telephone calls between him and the then RFU board chairman, Martyn Thomas, saved the day. Thomas, at the behest of the never-say-die scribe, facilitated a stay of execution pending a public appeal to raise the necessary funds, and although the £54,783 pledged over the next fortnight fell short of the full figure, Thomas and his RFU colleagues were sufficiently impressed to grant a green light, thereby ensuring that the club formed in 1874 would have a chance to rebuild.

Coventry were not out of the woods yet, however, with a further bout of financial difficulty and relegation to the third tier of English rugby following in season 2009–10. But after that the right people took charge and, led by club stalwart Peter Rossborough and current chairman Jon Sharp, a gradual rebuilding process means the club is on target to become a force once again.

Promotion from National League One last season means Coventry return to the Championship for the first time in eight years, and a decade on from nearly joining Orrell and Wakefield in becoming victims of the professional era by folding, the Butts Park Arena is now a vibrant place.

Sharp, 70, who remembers being taken by his father to Coventry's atmospheric old Coundon Road ground as a six-year-old and has remained faithful ever since, explained: 'I provided some early financial support and became a shareholder in the closed season in 2010, also joining the board of directors before becoming chairman in 2012. The task then was firstly one of consolidation, developing firm business foundations to support the planned resurgence of the club.

'This was initially very challenging in an environment where the club had bled away a lot of trust in the city and in the rugby community itself. That trust was gradually restored and with the help of many volunteers and sponsors the club got under way again, reaching third place in National One three years ago before a very inconsistent performance in 2015–16.

'On the playing front, I then took the plunge and signed up an aspiring 31-year-old as director of rugby and gave him his head. In two years Rowland Winter has built a very strong squad backed by a first-class support group of physios, strength and conditioners and support staff. After an initial few games finding our way, the club enjoyed a 25-game unbeaten run at the Butts Park Arena and last season went on to clinch promotion with five games in hand.

'Off the pitch we had been hampered by not having ownership of the undeveloped land surrounding the stand and pitch at the Butts Park Arena. So, in 2017, I completed, on behalf of the club, the purchase of the lease for this space, putting the whole nine-acre site back in the club's control. We engaged architects earlier this year to carry out an in-depth study of what could be done to develop the existing facilities and to envisage future new ones.'

So far so good, and despite the proximity of Premiership giants Wasps, who relocated from High Wycombe to the Ricoh Arena in December 2014, Coventry have progressed sufficiently to be in a position to plan for a

top-flight future of their own, with the ambitious target of meeting the Premiership's exacting stadium criteria over the next couple of years.

Sharp insists this is realistic, adding: 'The start point will be an artificial pitch, which we hope to put down next summer and which will help us expand our community programme, and we want indoor sporting facilities. You can't run a business on 15 home games a year and we have Coventry Bears Rugby League and Coventry United FC, along with their ladies team, playing at the ground, so we'd be better able to use our facilities year round, involving schools as well.

'We need a sustainable business so I'm also looking at some complementary commercial development on the site which would provide ongoing income.

'We've held discussions with a number of companies, which involve housing and retail, plus the aim is to build another stand and a standing terrace to replicate the old Cowshed at Coundon Road, and there's no reason why this can't all be done within two years.'

Sharp aims to replicate the successful model employed by Exeter Chiefs, explaining: 'We're looking for a maximum capacity of around 12,000 so that we can meet Premiership standards and I don't see why that shouldn't be amongst our longer-term ambitions.

'We attracted a crowd of just under 4,000 for our last match in National One and provided meals for 800 people, so that shows the scale of catering we can do and tells me we can take a punt on investing in more bars and hospitality facilities for our supporters.

'The only thing that concerns me is that only one Premiership club made any money last year, but I've always had an eye on Exeter's model where they've done a brilliant job by building everything step by step

LEFT Leaders of the Coventry technical staff, director of rugby Rowland Winter (right) and head coach Nick Walshe, look over a training session.

RIGHT Fly-half Will Maisey makes a break during the 38–21 victory over Hull Ionians that rounded off Coventry's successful League 1 campaign.

BELOW LEFT Tighthead prop Phil Boulton, seen at work during the summer 2018 pre-season, is to continue as club captain for 2018–19.

and not doing anything they couldn't afford.

'The trick is to secure those income streams and then we can assess where we want to be, but why should there be any limits to our ambition? We've been a top-flight club before so if we can afford it and think it's the right thing to do in future, why not?'

Off-field success needs backing up on it as well, and to that end rugby director Winter has been busy. Since promotion was assured in March, Coventry have recruited some high-class individuals, with former Gloucester wing David Halaifonua, ex-London Irish hooker Darren Dawidiuk and scrum-half Tom Kessell and back rower Ben Nutley (both Northampton) joining from the Premiership, along with Championship campaigners such as Tongan Test flanker Jack Ram, from Doncaster, and experienced ex-Yorkshire Carnegie prop Charlie Beech.

Winter, who joined from Cambridge in 2016, said: 'To finally get promoted brought a mixture of relief and elation. We brought in plenty of new faces last year and had lots of things to change, but that showed in our results and we're happy with our planning for this season.

'We've retained 85–90 per cent of our squad and did a lot of our recruitment early, meaning we've added a bit more depth and quality to meet the demands of the Championship. We kept a pretty close eye on that league last year and know that physically it will be a big step up.'

Winter is confident Coventry can thrive, adding: 'The club's developed massively over these last couple of years and we've got a development team starting up as well, which will improve our ability to produce our own players. We're enjoying some pretty good crowds too.

'People are excited about wanting to get involved in Coventry Rugby Club again and it's a good place to be. Rather than hindering us, the arrival of Wasps has raised the exposure of rugby in the city and that's had a good knock-on effect for us. We've got good coaches in Nick Walshe and Louis Deacon and we're confident we can make an impact in this season's Championship.'

If Coventry can hit their targets, both on and off the field, and arrive at a position where they can mount another promotion push, it would represent a remarkable turnaround for one of the biggest names in English rugby – a club that nearly went to the wall but survived.

Sharp, who makes his money leasing jet engines to the world's leading airlines, believes they are ready to soar. He said: 'My dad took me to Coundon Road when I was little and I always remember the atmosphere at that ground. It's something that's stayed with me and I'd like to re-create that at Butts Park Arena and make this one of the best clubs in the land again.

'We've done well during the closed season; there's a buzz about Coventry at the moment and with the coaches and professional set-up we've got, there's been a lot of interest from players who might not otherwise have thought about joining a club coming up from National One.

'That's hugely encouraging and, in my opinion, there are no limits to what this club can achieve. We're in a fantastic city-centre location and there's a lot of goodwill towards us now – all we have to do is to ensure that we put the right plans in place to fulfil our potential.'

Another Irish Triumph
THE EUROPEAN CHAMPIONS CUP

by DAVID HANDS

The competition also provided one of the best redemptive stories in rugby ... Lancaster was taken on board and the first thing he told the Leinster squad was: 'I think we can do great things here.'

Seldom have Irish eyes smiled more than they did last season but the widest grin belonged to Leinster. In becoming champions of Europe for the fourth time – they won in 2009, 2011 and 2012 – they dispatched the best clubs in the competing countries before winning an arm-wrestle against Racing 92 in Bilbao, the first occasion on which Spain has hosted the European Champions Cup final.

Look at the quality which fell to Leinster: Exeter Chiefs, the English champions, were beaten twice in pool play and they were followed by Saracens (who went on to oust Exeter as domestic champions) in the quarter-finals. Montpellier, the latest French club to ooze money and subsequently become Top 14 finalists, were beaten home and away in pool play and Scarlets, Wales' best hope and Guinness Pro14 champions, were thrashed in the semi-final stage.

That is a considerable list of battle honours and serves to emphasise how good a fist the Irish have made of professional rugby. Their rivals may not like it, and often say so, but careful inter-weaving of international

ABOVE Mathieu Bastareaud of Toulon during the Champions Cup match between Toulon and Treviso, 14 January 2018. Bastareaud was cited for misconduct after this match.

LEFT Nathan Hughes of Wasps hands off the tackle of Kevin Gourdon during Wasps' home European Champions Cup match with La Rochelle, December 2017.

demands with the European and domestic programme, which allows for the better management of leading players, carried Ireland in 2017–18 to second place in the world rankings, behind New Zealand.

Nor did Leinster neglect local talent. The starting XV for the 15–12 win against Racing contained just two overseas players, Isa Nacewa and Scott Fardy. Of those, Nacewa (playing his penultimate match before retirement) gave such long and unstinting service to the province that he was virtually Irish by adoption.

The competition also provided one of the best redemptive stories in rugby: Stuart Lancaster, cast aside as England head coach after a disastrous 2015 World Cup campaign, still had no permanent role in September 2016. But when Kurt McQuilkin, Leinster's defence coach, was forced by family reasons to return to New Zealand at short notice, Lancaster was taken on board and the first thing he told the Leinster squad was: 'I think we can do great things here.'

Given that he arrived after a season in which Leinster had finished stone last in their European pool, Lancaster's confidence was catching. He helped the province to the 2017 semi-finals, then last season's title, and now the Englishman in the Irish camp has become part of the furniture, alongside the head coach, Leo Cullen, who made some pointed observations before the start of the European campaign.

In particular Cullen, now the only man to have won the tournament as player and coach, emphasised that Leinster's was a 'sustainable model', in comparison with the financial losses of Saracens, Champions Cup winners in 2016 and 2017. 'We can't control what other teams do, we can't accumulate 50 million Euros of losses,' Cullen said. But whatever his budget, Cullen and his players have become a dominant force in rolling out an unbeaten 2017–18 European tally.

It started with an odd-looking back division against Montpellier at the RDS Arena: Johnny Sexton, Ireland's fly half and controlling genius, was missing, Joey Carbery, his deputy, was at full back, Ross Byrne at fly half and Nacewa, usually a wing, at centre. Nevertheless they prevailed 24–17 then went and did a number on Glasgow Warriors at Scotstoun.

Exeter, fresh from wins over Glasgow and away to Montpellier, had not lost on their home ground, Sandy Park, for a year when Leinster rolled into the West Country. But the Chiefs were forced into a prodigious number of errors and lost 18–8 on a weekend when all the English clubs playing in Europe lost.

Exeter believed, though, that they had learned enough to win in Dublin a week later and, when they led 17–3 and Leinster had lost Sexton to concussion, their belief seemed justified. But Nacewa, taking over as goalkicker, landed five penalties and Dan Leavy dispatched Luke McGrath to the try line for the score that gave Leinster their 22–17 win and virtually assured a quarter-final place.

The subsequent wins over Glasgow and Montpellier confirmed the last-eight meeting with the reigning champions, Saracens. The London club had come through a grim mid-winter period during which they were routed at home 46–14 by Clermont Auvergne (thereby ending an unbeaten 20-match run) and lost the return 24–21 to a long-range penalty from Scott Spedding. Indeed, Saracens won only three of their pool games and sneaked into the quarter-finals after the final qualifying round thanks to Wasps beating Ulster.

At least they qualified. In the Aviva Premiership's worst performance for six years, no other English team did, reflecting the decline of the national side. Leicester, Northampton and Harlequins were bottom of their respective pools, Leicester – once feared across Europe – taking a savage beating 39–0 in Castres, who went on to become Top 14 champions.

In contrast France, in their best showing since 2011, topped two pools through La Rochelle and Clermont; Toulon came second in pool five, likewise Racing 92 – flying below the radar at this stage – in pool four. This represented a splendid achievement by La Rochelle, playing in the tournament for the first time; their best

display was the 49–29 win over Wasps, six tries to the home side and five to the visitors who got something of their own back in Coventry a week later.

Clermont's only pool loss came, surprisingly, at Northampton who struggled so badly in domestic games as well as in Europe. Perhaps the six tries they scored on the visit to Saracens gave the French club delusions of grandeur but Northampton, inspired by Ben Foden in his last season with the club, won 34–21.

Toulon, champions in three successive seasons from 2013, spent much of the campaign living on the edge. They led Scarlets 18–0 in their opening match yet were clinging to a 21–20 win by the end. Another one-point win followed at Treviso before a 24–20 win over Bath, to whom they lost a week later in a match where Anthony Watson scored two tries for the English club. A comfortable 36–0 home win over Treviso was soured when Mathieu Bastareaud was cited for addressing a homophobic comment to an opponent, Sebastian Negri. It cost the France centre a three-week suspension and the matter was not helped when Mourad Boudjellal, Toulon's owner, added in the media his own comments on the matter and provoked a misconduct charge from the tournament organisers.

Toulon did their best to put such problems behind them against the Scarlets but the Welsh club won a nail-biting match 30–27 to secure a knockout place for the first time since 2007 and, importantly, a home tie. Conversely, Toulon had to play their quarter-final away to Munster, who were appearing in the last eight for a record 17th time.

Munster had occupied the same pool as Racing, both clubs going about their European business with an air of quiet solidity. The Paris-based club were beaten finalists in 2016 but have no great European tradition; their pool campaign, though, ended with a 23–20 win over Leicester at Welford Road, which buoyed them for the knockout game at injury-hit Clermont where they won 28–17.

La Rochelle's passionate journey ended at Parc y Scarlets when Leigh Halfpenny banged over five penalties to help Scarlets to a 29–17 win. But the fireworks were reserved for Ireland: with four minutes left on the Thomond Park clock, Munster were trailing Toulon by six points when François Trinh-Duc missed touch for Toulon. The ball was collected by Andy Conway and the wing slalomed his way through a startled defence for the try which, with Ian Keatley's conversion, won the game 20–19.

ABOVE Leone Nakawara of Racing 92 is tackled by James Tracy and Jack McGrath during the Champions Cup Final. Nakawara played every minute of all of Racing's games throughout the tournament.

ABOVE LEFT Scrum half Luke McGrath of Leinster gets his pass away during the final.

RIGHT Leinster head coach Leo Cullen (facing camera) is congratulated by Leinster head of rugby operations Guy Easterby following their team's win in Bilbao.

Meanwhile what of Leinster? Two weeks after Ireland had won the Grand Slam by beating England at Twickenham, the Irish province ended the two-year European reign of Saracens with a 30–19 win at the Aviva Stadium. The turning point came in a third quarter when Leinster scored 17 unanswered points, including tries by Leavy and James Lowe, and though Saracens kept fighting, there was to be no comeback.

Leinster kept their home advantage in the semi-finals and, led by Sexton with 18 points, they overwhelmed Scarlets 38–16. Five tries to one said it all, three of the Irish tries going to forwards whose ball-handling skills were of the highest quality. Even the solitary Scarlets try was scored by a former Leinster player, Tadgh Beirne, the lock who enjoyed an outstanding season in the red jersey though he plays in the red of Munster this season.

ABOVE Rob Kearney (left) and Jonathan Sexton of Leinster celebrate with the cup after the victory over Racing 92 in Bilbao.

Munster's semi-final was played in Bordeaux and when Racing had scored 21 points in 22 minutes, including two tries for Teddy Thomas on the wing, it seemed the journey had not agreed with Munster. But you can never take the fight out of the Irish province, even though their decision-making on the day was poor: in the last quarter they scored three tries, one of them to Simon Zebo who joined Racing in the summer, but Racing held on to reach the final with a 27–22 victory.

A crowd little short of capacity at the San Mamés Stadium saw Leinster reclaim the title in a slugfest. Gone the sweeping brilliance of the semi-final, instead five penalties – three by Sexton, two by Nacewa – earned the 15–12 win. Racing were without their injured presiding genius and goalkicker at scrum half, Maxime Machenaud, and lost their fly half, Patrick Lambie, after only three minutes.

But the replacements, Teddy Iribaren and Remi Tales, were outstanding with Iribaren kicking his side's four penalties. The game was won and lost in the last two minutes when Thomas tried to run from his own 22 and was ushered into touch; from there, Leinster won the line out, won an offside penalty and Nacewa kicked the decisive goal for a 15–12 victory.

Leavy, the flanker who was one of the finds of Ireland's season, made 20 tackles and 17 carries. Another of Leinster's new breed, James Ryan, the young lock, made a strong case for player of the tournament, an award which went instead to Racing's lock, Leone Nakarawa, who played all 720 minutes available.

When Leinster defend their title this season, it will be under the flag of an old friend to European rugby after Heineken, the Dutch brewers, agreed a four-year deal as title sponsors. The organisers, European Professional Club Rugby, have gone canton-hopping from Neuchâtel and will be based in Lausanne to oversee a tournament which remains the acme of the Northern Hemisphere club season.

Saracens on Top Again
THE AVIVA PREMIERSHIP

by CHRIS HEWETT

They will therefore be eternally grateful to the less garlanded members of the squad ... If Wray is often the only uncapped member of the Saracens starting line-up, you would be forgiven for not noticing.

I t would be a little hard on Exeter to suggest that they crashed and burned on Grand Final day at Twickenham, but they certainly came to earth with a resounding thump in losing 27–10 to a Saracens side of considerable quality, and much of the data contained in the deposed champions' black box will be profoundly alarming for Rob Baxter and his fellow coaches down there in deepest Devon. Not since the start of the 2016–17 campaign had Exeter suffered a more comprehensive defeat in Premiership rugby – Saracens inflicted the misery on that occasion, too – and they cannot have expected to finish as distant a second as they did.

Yet for those with eyes to see, there was always a possibility, however remote, that the West Countrymen would cop it if they ran into the wrong opponents on the wrong day: opponents blessed with more tactical flexibility, more attacking variety and sufficient energy and commitment to bring their defensive A-game to the fore. The indicators were provided by Leinster, who crossed the Irish Sea in the depths of winter for a European Champions Cup pool match and not only played Exeter at their own game – based around the three 'Ps' of possession, precision and patience – but played them off the park in the process. They effectively said to their hosts: 'If you want to go through 40 phases, fire away. We'll meet you head on, then go through 41 in return. We'll do more to you than you do to us, and we'll do it better. Let's see how YOU like it.'

Saracens did the same at Twickenham, yielding barely an inch as they stared down Exeter in the furious opening exchanges before taking things several stages further with ball in hand. Some of their work in open field was far beyond anything witnessed in their previous major finals, be they domestic or cross-border in nature, and had it not been for Baxter's intelligent use of his bench personnel in the 20 minutes after the interval, the Londoners might easily have registered another dozen points or more. It was a painful defeat for the 2017 winners because they knew they had been worked out. Without some meaningful adjustments – not a complete reinvention, maybe, but at the very least a meaningful attempt at renewal – there must be a danger that Exeter will head into the future as yesterday's men.

At the heart of the flowering of the Saracens attacking game in the second half of the season were England players present and past: Owen Farrell at outside-half and Alex Goode at full-back. For the very good reason that top-of-the-range, 24-carat inside centres are currently rarer than sightings of Lord Lucan riding Shergar into battle against Tolkienesque orcs mounted on demented unicorns, it is still possible to argue that Farrell is of

ABOVE Chris Robshaw of Harlequins takes on Nathan Hughes of Wasps during their early season clash at the Ricoh Stadium in Coventry. Quins won 24–21.

ABOVE LEFT Alex Goode of Saracens evades Henry Slade of Exeter Chiefs during the Premiership final at Twickenham.

LEFT Semesa Rokoduguni of Bath wrong-foots the Gloucester defence to score a late try during an October 2017 Premiership match. Gloucester won 22–21 after replying with a converted injury-time try of their own.

more use to England as a no. 12 than as a no. 10. But that argument is more difficult to sustain when his performance in the prime decision-making position is as complete as it was in the later stages of the Premiership. Rather like a half-decent stand off of yore by the name of Wilkinson, his kicking and tackling have always been to die for. Now that his distribution skills are on the rise and heading towards the same level, he is a very serious proposition indeed. He may well be the best player on the British mainland, in any position.

Goode, meanwhile, has become something of a lost soul in international terms. You might say he has been deliberately mislaid by the England head coach Eddie Jones, who, for some reason beyond the reach of mere mortal imagination, does not consider the most sophisticated creative spirit in the country to be of Test calibre. If Jones is right – if Goode's lack of extreme straight-line speed or his perceived lack of iron-man physicality automatically makes him surplus to requirements at the top end of the sport – then there is nothing to do except mourn. Without the kind of rugby intelligence displayed by Goode on a weekly basis, big-time rugby union is about as interesting as polenta. Heaven knows, we need some wit and wisdom to go with all the crashing and banging and walloping.

From the Saracens perspective, it was an odd campaign as well as a triumphant one. They started like a train, sticking nine tries past Northampton in an opening-day slaughter and then scoring 200 points, as near as damn it, in winning five of six games that followed. But when injuries and international calls kicked in, they disappeared into a maze from which they would not emerge for several painful weeks, running into months. The wing Sean Maitland, the centre Duncan Taylor, the scrum-half Richard Wigglesworth and any number of

forwards – Jamie George, Schalk Brits, Vincent Koch, Maro Itoje, George Kruis, Michael Rhodes, Schalk Burger, the unusually substantial Vunipola brothers, Mako and Billy . . . all of these and more were absent for long periods, for one reason or another. Only when the Six Nations was done and dusted did the elite side come together again, and by that time, there was work to be done.

They will therefore be eternally grateful to the less garlanded members of the squad – or, as in the case of the back-row forward Jackson Wray, the wholly ungarlanded ones, at least in Test terms. If Wray is often the only uncapped member of the Saracens starting line-up, you would be forgiven for not noticing. His protean ability to play across the loose unit makes him as important to the club as his great World Cup-winning predecessor Richard Hill, and if Wray is not quite the player Hill was, it is hardly a condemnation. The academy graduate won two versions of the Sarries 'Player of the Season' award – both his on-field colleagues and the supporters singled him out for gongs – and he deserved every last drop of the praise heaped upon him.

There were others up and down the land who performed minor heroics in adversity yet finished the season with their relative anonymity intact. One of Wray's back-row rivals, Jamie Gibson of Northampton, was borderline brilliant on a weekly basis, even though the 2014 champions were rarely anything better than dire in their descent towards the lower reaches of the table. Harlequins, making pretty much the same kind of journey south, had to throw Marcus Smith, a teenage playmaker barely out of swaddling clothes, into the big bad world outside the manger, and were relieved to see him survive, and then thrive. Not that Gibson and Smith could right all of the wrongs that surrounded them. Both Jim Mallinder and John Kingston, the directors of rugby at Saints and Quins respectively, lost their jobs before season's end.

There were similar football-style manoeuvrings in the human resources department at both Worcester, who flirted with relegation as per usual, and London Irish, who flirted just that little bit more seriously and found themselves disappearing through the trapdoor once again. Two old-stagers, the South African fixer Alan Solomons and the Irish strategist Declan Kidney, were promoted to fill the top jobs, but they will need more than a lifetime's accumulation of rugby knowledge to prosper. They will require access to all the modern conveniences of life in 21st-century rugby union, including large amounts of money. Who can say at this moment of great financial and economic uncertainty that they will be given it?

Despite the sharp improvement of Newcastle, who boasted the hardest-working back-five forward unit in the country together with a pair of sensational South Seas wings in Sinoti Sinoti and Vereniki Goneva, only Wasps had the equipment to pose a serious threat to the Premiership's two most obvious title contenders. Yet while some of their all-singing, all-dancing box-office attractions – Dan Robson, Willie le Roux, Christian Wade, Elliot Daly, the outstanding Danny Cipriani – succeeded in providing regular confirmations that rugby union is indeed the game they play in heaven, the Coventry-based team were just a little too brittle up front when the most difficult questions were asked, even though the open-side flanker Thomas Young repeatedly played the house down. Young cannot find a place in the Wales squad because there are as many as four no. 7s ahead of him. Justin Tipuric, Josh Navidi, James Davies, Ellis Jenkins . . . each and every one of them would have walked into the England team in the 2018 Six Nations. So too would Young. Extraordinary, but true.

It remains to be seen whether the Premiership clubs catch up in this department. A change of refereeing approach would surely help: only when a proper contest for the ball at the tackle area is permitted will an all-round flanker with a full armoury of skills hone his game sufficiently to make an impact on the Test scene. Two youngsters from fair-to-middling clubs, Sam Underhill of Bath and Tom Curry of Sale, have something about them on the evidence of the 2017–18 season, but they spent too long off the field nursing injuries to make the most of their gifts and on the odd occasion when they were fit, the breakdown rules cramped their style. A fresh approach is required. One that will, pray God, make 40-phase attacks a relic rather than a reality.

LEFT Marland Yarde breaks the tackle of Dave Denton during the Sale *v*. Worcester Premiership match, 24 March 2018.

BELOW Jonny May of Leicester Tigers tries to break free from the Northampton Saints defence during the late-season clash at Welford Road, won 27–21 by Saints.

Silverware for Cardiff Blues
THE EUROPEAN CHALLENGE CUP

by DAVID STEWART

'It's a fantastic feeling. For this group over a three-year period to go through the ups and downs they have, and finish off in style to win silverware is fantastic, something I'll always remember.'

The Cardiff (and Rhondda Valleys) region have history in this competition. In front of a crowd of almost 50,000, the largest ever for the tournament, they beat Toulon 28–21 in nearby Marseille at the end of the 2009–10 season. This time they crossed the Pyrenees to the San Mamés Stadium, Bilbao. In a performance which surprised the bookmakers and at least some of their supporters, the Blues beat Gloucester (the winners in 2015 and runners-up a year earlier) by a single point in injury time before 32,500 spectators – the second-highest in the history of the competition, perhaps an illustration of the wisdom in taking these finals to 'venue destinations'.

Prior to the imposition of regional rugby by the WRU in 2003, Cardiff (the Blue & Blacks) understandably considered themselves be one of the most significant club sides in the world. Bob Norster, then CEO, argued – with some logic – that, in commercial terms, the population of the greater Cardiff area justified them continuing as effectively a stand-alone entity in the evolving structure of the Welsh professional game. Ironically, the rugby politics of the time dictated that Cardiff be partnered with Pontypridd – who traditionally enjoyed a supply of players and much support from the famous Rhondda Fach and Fawr valleys to which that town is the gateway. It was a marriage of administrative convenience, and there were a few ironic smiles among senior Cardiff officials when their traditional rivals in the west – Llanelli – became the only independent or unmerged

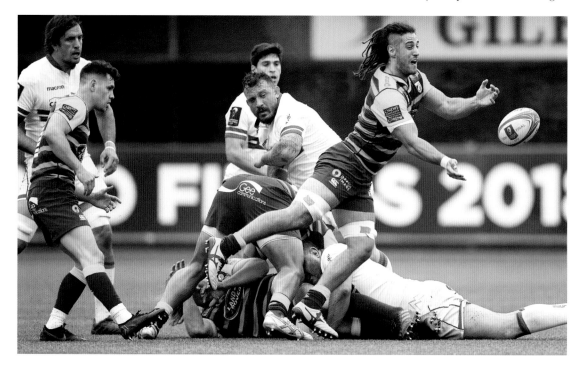

ABOVE Gareth Anscombe (right) and Nick Williams celebrate with the Challenge Cup trophy, San Mamés Stadium, 11 May 2018.

LEFT Blues flanker Josh Navidi gets an attack started during the Challenge Cup 16–10 semi-final win against Pau in Cardiff .

entity in the new regional structure, albeit with responsibility for mid and north Wales (from whence came the outstanding George North).

Cardiff appeared in the first ever European Cup final, losing to Toulouse at the old Wales National Stadium in January 1996. Since the European competition became two-tier, they have spent more years in the lower one than their pride would be comfortable with. That said, if you're in it, you might as well win it. So, the regional side having had its struggles in recent seasons – finances are not what they were, with an unhealthy turnover of head coaches, and consequently players, it was a wonderful boost to finish the 2017–18 season with their first trophy since that great win in the south of France eight years earlier.

Their campaign started with a home tie against Lyon. The French side have little pedigree beyond their domestic league, so it would not have been a surprise – as with other French teams in the past – to see them demonstrate less than full commitment in their European fixtures. Not so, as shown by a 29–19 score at Cardiff in October; the return fixture in late January saw the Blues victorious 18–21.

No sane observer has ever questioned how seriously Toulouse take European rugby. Since the departure of long-standing coach Guy Novès, they are not the force of old, clearly in a rebuilding phase. Nevertheless, it was a terrific achievement for the Blues to win their second fixture of the competition at the Stade Ernest-Wallon 15–17.

ABOVE Billy Burns of Gloucester (right) celebrates his try early in the second half of the Challenge Cup semi-final with Newcastle Falcons at Kingsholm.

RIGHT Cardiff Blues' centre Garyn Smith scores his team's second try in the final, assisted by New Zealander Willis Halaholo.

A disappointing December defeat to Sale at the A. J. Bell Stadium 24–0 was encouragingly reversed the following week at the Arms Park by 14–6. Come the new year, and Toulouse were beaten 18–13, with a second win over Lyon a week later at the Stade de Gerland (scene of the previous year's final) meaning five wins from six in their pool, and 21 points – a terrific achievement in the light of their fairly ordinary returns in the Pro14.

Their quarter-final draw was against Edinburgh at Murrayfield, where a fine performance saw the Blues triumph 6–20. This brought a home semi-final against Pau when the old Cardiff Arms Park club ground fitted in nearly 12,000 people, the biggest crowd of the season watching a 16–10 victory.

And so to the Basque country to take on their old rivals from across the Severn. After promising fly half Jarrod Evans put the Blues into the lead with an early penalty, his opposite number Billy Burns neatly measured a cross-kick for Henry Trinder to put Gloucester ahead.

The Blues lost Josh Navidi and right wing Owen Lane to injury early in the first half, and struggled for the remainder of that period. A well-constructed team try initiated by Billy Twelvetrees enabled centre Mark Atkinson to cross, their half-time lead of 20–6 putting the English club in a strong position.

A tactical switch after the interval – forgoing the choke tackle in favour of the chop – was effective for the Blues. Exciting scrum-half Tomos Williams – now a Welsh international with an eye on a regular place in the national match-day squad following the departure of Rhys Webb to Toulon – showed dribbling skills that would impress Ryan Giggs, before scoring by the posts. Evans kicked a third penalty before threading a clever grubber for Garyn Smith, the replacement for Lane, to touch down – albeit with a hint of offside: 23–20.

Next came a try by Gloucester's Australian hooker James Hanson, appearing to make the game safe for Johan Ackermann's team with a 10 point margin, at 30–20. All three of the Gloucester tries were converted by Twelvetrees, who had also kicked three penalties.

The closing stages saw the Blues lay siege to the Gloucester line and, as so often happens, a sin-bin offence – against flanker Lewis Ludlow (already unfortunate to have had a try disallowed by Jérôme Garcès, for a forward pass) – reduced the West Country team to 14 men. A third Blues try from left wing, the retiring US Eagles player Blaine Scully, closed the gap to 30–28. Anscombe could not manage the touchline conversion, but with less than a minute to go, he kicked a difficult penalty from the other side of the field to ensure the most unlikely of comeback victories – all this without the club's best-known player, Lions captain Sam Warburton.

The great back row forward – sadly now prematurely retired – was on a sabbatical, in an effort to allow his battered body to recover fully from more than one long-standing injury. Benefitting from his absence Oli Robinson, son of Andy, was deservedly named man-of-the match. The leadership role was ably filled by Eli

Jenkins (who went on to become co-captain on the Wales tour to the USA and Argentina), Navidi (who enjoyed the confidence of Warren Gatland throughout the Six Nations), and experienced second-row Josh Turnbull.

Their success came against a backdrop of a rather ordinary Pro14 campaign, and the planned departure of

ABOVE Billy Twelvetrees of Gloucester celebrates his team's third try, scored by James Hanson, in the Challenge Cup final. Gloucester couldn't hang on to their lead, however.

their interesting, resourceful and effective young head coach Danny Wilson – who is now assisting Gregor Townsend as Scotland's forwards coach. Wilson summed up the achievement thus: 'It's a fantastic feeling. For this group over a three-year period to go through the ups and downs they have, and finish off in style to win silverware is fantastic, something I'll always remember. In the second half we decided to play from deeper – that paid off.'

Retiring Chairman Peter Thomas is optimistic for the future: 'I have never seen a group of young players better than are coming through.' With Cardiff City restored to the Premier League of the round-ball game, in pure commercial terms it is important for the Blues to appeal to potential fans once again as a serious outfit that can win trophies, thus sending them into the new season with confidence and the right kind of optimism.

REVIEW OF THE SEASON 2017-18

5

Ireland – Europe's Best
THE SIX NATIONS CHAMPIONSHIP

by **CHRIS JONES**

That Sexton drop goal – the final act of the match in Paris – grabbed the headlines at the time but no one realised it would ultimately win the Slam.

Ireland lifted the NatWest Six Nations trophy at Twickenham to celebrate their country's third Grand Slam, a triumph that owed so much to a record-breaking seven-try campaign from wing Jacob Stockdale and a 41-phase move that ended with Johnny Sexton dropping a goal to defeat France on the opening weekend of the championship.

It was supposed to be England cast in the role of history-makers as Eddie Jones' men started the 2018 campaign bidding to become the first team to win the Six Nations three times in a row; but they would suffer three successive defeats to leave them second from bottom with only the winless Italians worse off.

BELOW Jonathan Sexton (right) and Bundee Aki celebrate Ireland's dramatic last-gasp victory in Paris.

RIGHT Teddy Thomas, France's try-scorer against Ireland during the opening round of the tournament.

That Sexton drop goal – the final act of the match in Paris – grabbed the headlines at the time but no one realised it would ultimately win the Slam and confirm Ireland as the most successful nation in the Northern Hemisphere, with Leinster claiming the European Champions Cup. It was reward for all the work Joe Schmidt, his fellow coaches and the players had delivered and only served to highlight how far England had slipped – something that was confirmed by their series loss in South Africa in the summer and a slump from no. 2 in the world rankings to no. 6.

It had started so well for England with Owen Farrell scoring 16 points as they eased to a 46–15 win over Italy in Rome. Anthony Watson and Sam Simmonds both scored two tries in their bonus-point win, with Tommaso Benvenuti crossing in the first half and Mattia Bellini in the second for the home side who were trying to end a run of Six Nations defeats that had started to bring into question their right to be in the championship when Georgia were pushing hard to gain entry.

It had been a totally different story in Paris where Sexton's drop goal gave his side a hard-fought 15–13 win over a French side under the control of new head coach Jacques Brunel, the ex-Italy coach. Teddy Thomas' try seemed to have given the French the win but Anthony Belleau missed a kick to give France a four-point lead and that allowed Sexton to emerge as the Irish hero.

If the Paris match was all about kicks, the opening quarter of Wales's home game with Scotland was all about pace. Wales scored tries through a Gareth Davies intercept and one by Leigh Halfpenny, and they held a 14–0 lead at half-time. Halfpenny, who scored 24 points, added two penalties and his second try with one from the athletic Steff Evans securing the bonus point. Scotland replied through Peter Horne who gave Scotland a late try, but Wales coach Warren Gatland continued his record of not having lost to Scotland.

Stockdale grabbed two tries at the start of a marvellous run for the wing and there was also a brace for centre Robbie Henshaw as Ireland eased to an eight-try 56–19 victory over Italy in Dublin. The Irish had wrapped up a bonus point by half time and, while Italy were never going to win, they came close to a try bonus point only for Keith Earls to deny Bellini the crucial score.

The England win over Wales was marred by a TMO mistake with Gareth Anscombe being denied a try as he got his hand to the ball before the English cover, but it was ruled out and Eddie Jones' men claimed a 12–6 win to keep their hopes of making history alive. It was a bitter pill for Wales to swallow. They could not stop Jonny May claiming his first tries in the championship in the opening 20 minutes of a torrid battle in tough conditions. Wales were denied another score by one of the best try-saving tackles ever seen at Twickenham as Sam Underhill got just enough of Scott Williams to drag him into touch.

Scotland hosted France at Murrayfield on a day that signalled Greig Laidlaw's return after 12 months out of the side. He responded with 22 points from his trusty right boot to cancel out a French challenge which included two first-half tries from Teddy Thomas, proving to be a handful for every defence. Sean Maitland and Huw Jones scored tries but it was Laidlaw's boot that was responsible for the 32–26 win.

After two defeats, France needed some inspiration and it came in the bulky form of centre Mathieu Bastareaud who was the star in Marseille in a Friday night game on the south coast. Both sides scored tries from driving mauls and, despite lots of chances, the home side only led 11–7 at half time. However, in the second half Bastareaud created the chance for Hugo Bonneval to score and then claimed one of his own to end a run of eight defeats for the French while the Italians were left to reflect on a 34–17 loss which only increased the pressure on coach Conor O'Shea.

The predatory skills of left wing Stockdale were evident once again in Dublin as he grabbed a brace to give Ireland a 37–27 win in a breathless contest with a Welsh side that just would not give up. Stockdale and Bundee Aki scored first half tries for the Irish while scrum half Gareth Davies raced in under the posts for the Welsh. It appeared the Irish pack had done enough to earn the win when Aaron Shingler and Steff Evans suddenly scored tries for Wales, who thus got to within three points of the hosts with just a few minutes of the pulsating game to play. As they chased glory, Gareth Anscombe sent out a long pass and Stockdale intercepted to race to the posts and Joey Carbery converted.

While Ireland maintained their unbeaten record, England's came to an abrupt end against Scotland at Murrayfield where they fell 25–13 thanks to excellent tries from Huw Jones (2) and Sean Maitland. Maitland's was created initially by a magical, floated pass into space by Finn Russell, who had been heavily criticised before the match but delivered a stunning performance. England fought back but saw Sam Underhill yellow-carded to undermine their cause and any Slam and Triple Crown hopes were ended as the Scots claimed the Calcutta Cup for the first time in ten years.

The fourth round of fixtures would end with the Irish confirmed as champions thanks to their 28–8 win over

ABOVE Jacob Stockdale of Ireland about to ground his first-half try under pressure from Leigh Halfpenny of Wales. Stockdale's last-minute interception score in the second half sealed the Irish victory.

ABOVE RIGHT Maxime Machenaud during France's win over England. Machenaud was the tournament's top scorer.

RIGHT Wales' wing George North runs through to score one of his two tries against Italy.

Scotland as England were beaten in Paris. Yet again, Stockdale collected a brace of tries as his team gained a bonus point win totally to deflate the Scots. Conor Murray and Sean Cronin also scored tries for the Irish with Blair Kinghorn replying for the visitors, who should have scored another when Huw Jones burst through but then failed to give the ball to the supporting Stuart Hogg.

It was another defeat for faltering England as they crashed 22–16 at the Stade de France, having gone into the game knowing that only a bonus-point win could stop the Irish from taking the title. Jonny May got another impressive try for England but the home side created enough mayhem to earn a penalty try and with five more

Our *global* hunters scour the map for hidden PROFITS.

When Profits are scarce in one part of the world, they can often abound elsewhere. That's why our global hunters spend their lives carving through the atlas. Relying on their keen eyes and sharp reactions to bag far-flung Profits that others have failed to find. Leaving no stone – or page – unturned.

ARTEMIS
The PROFIT Hunter

0800 092 2051   *investorsupport@artemisfunds.com*   *artemisfunds.com*

penalties kicked through the posts, the reigning champions were left to rue their poor discipline as the French celebrated an important scalp.

The sight of the returning George North gave Welsh fans something to cheer and they were on their feet twice as he raced over for scores in the 38–14 win over Italy to earn Gatland's team second place in the table with one

round of matches to go. James Davies made his Welsh debut in a side captained by Taulupe Faletau whose team gave him a bonus-point start in the role. Centre Hadleigh Parkes was outstanding, scoring the first try while Cory Hill went over early in the second half. Italy were quickly 14–0 down but scored through Matteo Minozzi with Tommaso Allan converting. Liam Williams was yellow-carded but Wales still created a try while he was off the pitch. Scrum half Davies also went into the bin and Italy scored a second try through Mattia Bellini .

Italy finished their campaign by coming agonisingly close to a much-needed win, having led the Scots 24–12 only to fall 29–27 to a late Laidlaw kick. Tommaso Allan, who played for Scotland Under-18s, scored 19 points but it wasn't enough as the Azzuri suffered a 17th successive loss in the Six Nations. There were signs of improvement from the home side with Gloucester's Jake Polledri setting up a try for Allan but it was not enough as Maitland and Hogg also scored tries.

All eyes then turned to Twickenham. Any thoughts that the Irish would struggle to cope with the weight of expectation against England ended as they scored first half tries through Garry Ringrose, CJ Stander and Stockdale. Elliot Daly claimed a brace for England who suffered their first home defeat in the championship since 2012. Peter O'Mahony pulled down a maul and was given a yellow card which helped Daly get his first try only for Conor Murray to settle nerves with a long-range penalty, and even though May scored late on for the English, the win and the Slam were already in the bag.

While the Irish were turning Twickenham green, Wales were edging out France 14–13 as the visitors missed kicks that would have given them victory. Instead it was Wales who finished second in the table thanks to Halfpenny's boot and a try from Liam Williams .

The Club Scene
ENGLAND: BRISTOL BACK AGAIN

by NEALE HARVEY

'Players in Premiership academies need to play, I understand that, but what the RFU and Premiership Rugby are doing undermines the core values of sportsmanship and respect.'

It was all change as far as the RFU Championship was concerned, with the annual end of season play-offs – cursed by ambitious clubs with big-money backers, beloved by lesser brethren concerned only with extending their seasons and causing some reputational damage along the way – being scrapped in favour of the first-past-the-post system that had been discarded in 2009.

In an ironic twist, it was Bristol who benefitted most from the change.

On five occasions the West Country club, backed by Steve Lansdown's billions, had reached the damned play-offs, but only once had they prevailed – in 2016, when they finally crawled over the line after being denied in 2010, 2012, 2014 and 2015. As money-wasting exercises go, Bristol will not look upon that period with fondness, and few people could argue with them.

However, with sanity finally prevailing, Bristol, who had suffered an immediate return to the second tier in 2016–17, set about the campaign with renewed vigour, moving out of the reach of nearest challengers Ealing Trailfinders to clinch the title with three games to spare, thus affording them a far better chance of preparing for their latest top-flight campaign.

Bristol – now known as the 'Bears' after a controversial rebranding – have no intention of making a rapid return this time. Chris Booy, their chairman, said bullishly: 'Since the game went professional we have not done well. We've yo-yoed between the Premiership and the Championship three or four times, been close to bankruptcy three times and generally failed to compete. 'But we're confident we're past all that and whilst we want to keep all our existing fans, we want younger fans to get behind us and fill Ashton Gate. Those younger people get the 'Bears' rebranding and there's real expectation around this club now.

'Joe Public might think we're going to struggle but we don't think we are and we'll see fans coming in good numbers. We had 14,000 for our last Championship game so we'll aim for 18,000 next season and if we can get to 20,000, then great. With all the local derbies against Exeter, Bath, Gloucester and Worcester, if we can get into the upper end of the table we might even regularly exceed that.'

Good luck Bristol; results will be the judge.

Elsewhere in the Championship, there was fantastic news for Penzance-based Cornish Pirates, who overcame an early season blip to finish fourth and, way more importantly, received news that the long-awaited Stadium for Cornwall in Truro would finally be built. To say people have grown old waiting for this news is an understatement, but it is a game-changer as far as the Pirates are concerned and it means the ring-fencing brigade who would close off the Premiership and be done with the rest must quell their bilious voices.

As Exeter proved a decade ago, a pathway for ambitious clubs must remain and who is to say that in another ten years the Pirates won't be parading the Premiership trophy around Cornwall? Their long-serving back row, Chris Morgan, 36, said: 'Time is running out for me and I'm unlikely to play at the new stadium, but the boost of knowing the stadium will finally be built is fantastic.

'You always believed it would happen eventually, but to reach the Championship final against London Welsh in 2012 knowing we couldn't go up was frustrating, so the fact we can go for it properly in the near future is great for everyone here. Seeing what Exeter have done is inspirational and the stadium will be there for us to attract players. If the opportunity then arises where we're strong enough, we can go for promotion knowing that this time we can get there.'

Ealing and Bedford filled the remaining top four places, but there was disappointment for perennial strugglers Rotherham, whose parlous financial state finally overwhelmed them and they were relegated after winning just two matches to finish 26 points behind London Scottish. College side Hartpury finished a creditable 10th in their first season in the second tier, while part-timers Richmond continued to confound by finishing ninth – a place higher than 2016–17.

LEFT Rhodri Williams of Bristol Rugby is tackled by Josh Tyrell during Bristol's 68–10 win against Doncaster Knights on 13 April 2018.

BELOW LEFT Pat Lam, Bristol head coach, poses with the Championship trophy along with fellow Samoan David Lemi following the Doncaster game.

RIGHT Skipper of Cornish Pirates Nicolas De Battista about to score a try in Pirates' 34–29 away victory over Bedford Blues in the second-last week of the league season.

In National League One, Coventry romped home by 19 points from Darlington Mowden Park, winning promotion to the Championship with three games to spare, while revitalised Plymouth Albion and Ampthill both topped the 100-point mark in finishing third and fourth. Little known Kent outfit Old Elthamians achieved great things in their first season at level three by finishing sixth – remember their name for they have big ambitions. The real drama in the division came at the bottom, however, where Hull Ionians were relegated in controversial fashion.

A change in regulations at the start of the season meant National One clubs could field as many as ten England Academy Players from Premiership clubs, plus an additional three 'loan' players on top, which afforded Loughborough Students the opportunity to tie up with Leicester Tigers. The two near neighbours had always enjoyed a relationship, but the Students cashed in to such good effect in a difficult season that they survived by three points, with Ionians demoted instead.

Efforts over the summer to amend the regulations have failed, meaning another side could suffer a similar fate this season. Ionians rugby director Martyn Wood lamented: 'Players in Premiership academies need to play, I understand that, but what the RFU and Premiership Rugby are doing undermines the core values of sportsmanship and respect. The costs associated with keeping a club in National One are substantial and it takes a huge effort from sponsors, players and coaches and everyone involved, so to have Premiership Rugby dictating leaves a bad taste. I know the idea is to get young academy lads playing senior men's rugby but it shouldn't be at the cost of the whole of community rugby or the integrity of the leagues as a whole. It's not inclusive, it's a disaster. Relegation has cost us sponsors and players have now left us because, quite understandably, they want to keep playing in National One.'

You have to sympathise with Wood, whose side were accompanied into National Two by Old Albanians and Fylde.

Sale edged a thrilling National Two North title race to win promotion ahead of Sedgley Park by a single point over the 30-match campaign, but affairs were far more clear-cut in National Two South where Cinderford

comfortably held off Chinnor to return to National One. Chinnor then hosted Sedgley Park in a play-off for the final promotion spot and prevailed 40–31 in a thriller to take their place in the third tier, which was tough luck on their gallant northern visitors.

Blaydon, Luctonians and Sheffield were relegated from National Two North, while Barnstaple, Wimbledon and Broadstreet bowed out in the South. They will be replaced by Barnes, Birmingham & Solihull, Preston Grasshoppers, Dings Crusaders, Peterborough Lions and Guernsey, with the latter further closing the gap on traditional Channel Island rivals Jersey, who they went on to defeat 46–30 in the keenly contested annual Siam Cup clash at their packed Footes Lane stadium.

Guernsey do not intend resting on their laurels as they chase down their Championship neighbours. Chairman Charlie McHugh said: 'We've come up seven leagues and we've got a good stadium and one of the bigger crowds in the league, so although the financial implications are quite scary, we do have a plan to deal with promotion. What we can say is that we're one of the most popular destinations for away teams to visit, so National Two will benefit from that.'

Bristol-based Dings Crusaders also harbour bold ambitions after opening the doors to a new £7.2m stadium, and Peterborough Lions are making plans for a further promotion assault. Roger Moyle, their ultra-positive director of rugby, said: 'Peterborough's a big city with a population of over 180,000 and whilst Peterborough United FC have always held sway, all of a sudden we're amongst the top 72 rugby clubs in the country and that should bolster things.

'We can attract extra sponsorship, get businesses involved and local players now have an ambitious National League club with good facilities they can play for without having to travel to the likes of Cambridge, Ampthill or Leicester Lions. I'd hope young, ambitious players would join us now and get good coaching and a good style of rugby in a team which, hopefully, will compete next year. We don't want to be a yo-yo outfit, we want to build to National One.'

Lower league cup competitions continue to enthral, with a day out at Twickenham the prize, and finals day this year saw Camberley lift the prestigious RFU Intermediate Cup, thrashing Droitwich 63–14 in a one-sided affair, while Wath Upon Dearne prevailed 22–18 over Saltash in the RFU Senior Vase and Old Otliensians captured the RFU Junior Vase, defeating South Molton 32–21.

County Championship finals day saw Lancashire lift the Bill Beaumont Cup after defeating Hertfordshire 32–16 at Twickenham, while Durham claimed the Plate 46–12 over Warwickshire.

SCOTLAND: THE CITIES AND THE SUPER SIX

by ALAN LORIMER

This elite pathway may be the answer for Scotland to keep up with the international pack but if the grassroots are not tended then the feeder system will suffer.

After luxuriating in a plethora of plaudits over the past few seasons Glasgow Warriors woke up to find they now have serious competition for these accolades from their East Coast rival and perennial underperformers, Edinburgh.

The capital club desperately needed a motivational figure to whip it into shape and in Englishman Richard Cockerill, Edinburgh found the right ringmaster. Cockerill's uncompromising training, that would have made Marine recruits weep, infused his charges with a new hard edge that for the most part translated into a decent set of results in the Guinness Pro14.

Cockerill's coaching career, it will be recalled, appeared to have stalled when he parted company with his home club, Leicester Tigers, following a slump in fortunes at Welford Road. A move to Toulon proved to be a temporary measure for Cockerill, who was swiftly snapped up by a Scottish Rugby Board desperate to effect a sea change at Edinburgh.

For too long Edinburgh Rugby had lived up to the capital's reputation of middle-class gentility, that so often resulted in style over substance, or, as they used to say in Auld Reekie: 'Fur coats and nae knickers.'

From being perceived as regular failures in the then Pro12 – they finished ninth in the previous season – Edinburgh suddenly emerged as a competitive team, confirming their new-found form by winning the best-of-three matches against Glasgow Warriors.

In fact Edinburgh matched Glasgow in the 2017–18 season with 15 wins in the Guinness Pro14 Conference 'B', and at the end of the league proper they were just two points behind the eventual winners, Leinster. Edinburgh's performances secured

ABOVE RIGHT (Left to right) Jonny Gray of Glasgow Warriors and opposite numbers Grant Gilchrist and Ben Toolis wrestle in a maul during Glasgow's 17–0 victory on 30 December 2017.

LEFT Glasgow Warriors head coach Dave Rennie (R) and Richard Cockerill of Edinburgh share a lighter moment as they return to the ground after a fire alarm during the 30 December match.

the capital club a place in the Guinness Pro14 play-offs only for them to lose to Munster in the semi-final qualifier.

This result, part of a late season dip, was evidence that Cockerill's transformation work is barely half completed, amplified by Edinburgh's home defeat to Cardiff Blues in the quarter-final of the European Challenge Cup, a competition in which Edinburgh had promised much with pool victories over Stade Français, Krasny Yar and London Irish that resulted in Edinburgh finishing group winners with five wins from six matches.

The new coaching regime stamped its mark on the club with refreshing selection calls, the principal beneficiaries of which were winger Dougie Fife, who regained recognition after being shunned by the previous management, back rows Magnus Bradbury and Jamie Richie, second row Grant Gilchrist and full back Blair Kinghorn.

The season also confirmed the potential of two South Africans, Duhan van der Merwe, a big and strong-running winger in the mould of George North, and fly-half Jaco van der Walt, both likely to become Scotland-qualified, having arrived in Edinburgh before the three-year residency door was slammed shut. Another player to star for Edinburgh was the Fijian sevens Olympic gold medallist, Vili Mata, who brought a blend of subtle attacking skills and raw strength to the back row.

Ultimately what put a ceiling on Edinburgh's achievements was the same factor that limited Glasgow Warriors in realising their ambitions: that with only two professional clubs north of the border each loses a higher-than-average number of players to the national set-up, compared to major clubs in other countries.

The welcome improvement by Edinburgh, however, could not overshadow the achievements of a Glasgow Warriors side, which, under the stewardship of New Zealander, Dave Rennie, set a ferocious pace in the Pro14, losing only one game in the first sixteen league matches to open a massive lead in Conference 'A' before a combination of injuries and fatigue allowed the chasing pack to narrow but not close Warriors' points advantage.

Rennie's style was similar to that of his predecessor at Glasgow, Gregor Townsend. Glasgow, helped by having an artificial pitch, played a joyously open brand of rugby that thrilled the Scotstoun crowd. But, having stormed the Guinness Pro14, Glasgow Warriors were decidedly becalmed in European Cup rugby after losing home and away to Leinster and Montpellier and away to Exeter to finish bottom of their group.

Glasgow's hopes of any European success were shot to pieces in their opening match against Exeter when the Scotstoun-based team were hugely outmuscled, exposing a weakness in the Warriors' forward make-up that was to cost them dearly in their European campaign. The brutal truth is that Glasgow, and to an extent Edinburgh, do not have the combined ballast up front to take on the beefy sides in the Aviva Premiership or the Top 14 across the Channel. Importing massive forward power is an option but that does not fit the purpose of Scotland's professional sides, which is essentially to develop players for the national team.

In which context Glasgow can be pleased by the emergence of scrum half George Horne and Matt Fagerson, whose respective elder brothers Peter and Zander are established Warriors. Other players to impress were hookers George Turner, who optimised his 'loan' move from Edinburgh, and former Glasgow Hawks front row Grant Stewart, who showed that talented players can make the jump from the amateur game to professional rugby.

Further development of home-grown players at both Glasgow and Edinburgh will be necessary following the moves by Finn Russell (to Racing 92) and Sam Hidalgo-Clyne (to Scarlets) but that is the *raison d'être* of the two Scottish clubs.

The two-club situation in Scotland also makes it difficult to accommodate the rising numbers of skilful players coming through Scottish Rugby's regional academies, one reason why Murrayfield introduced its so-called Super Six franchise clubs, which, according to Scottish Rugby, should narrow the gap between professional and 'amateur' rugby.

Each Super Six club will support a squad of up to 35 part-time professionals and will play in a closed competition, supplemented by cross-border matches. But, given the meagre amount of money on offer to these part-timers (£12k is the stated maximum), calling them professionals is taking something of a descriptive liberty. Indeed some wags have already quipped that 'amateurs' will take a wage cut by becoming part-time professionals.

At the end of a bidding process into which amateur clubs were invited, the 'lucky' winners were Melrose, Heriot's, Watsonians, Boroughmuir, Ayr and Stirling, in a stroke turning these famous names in Scottish rugby and bastions of a bygone amateur age into new semi-professional creatures. The skewed geographic distribution of the selection with half of the Super Six based in Edinburgh and none in Glasgow has caused discontent within the Scottish rugby community, mollified by Murrayfield's hints that the franchise could be increased from six to eight clubs.

While securing a franchise may be something of a coup for the successful bidders the cost to them will be a loss of autonomy. Murrayfield will have a major say in the appointment of head coaches and of the ancillary staff necessary to run these supernova clubs. A further uncertainty is whether the new Super Six clubs will have the finances to pay their share of the not inconsiderable wages bill when the new set-up kicks off in the 2019–20 season.

Ambitious clubs like Melrose and Ayr, it seemed to outsiders, were already semi-professional in their approach to driving up standards. Melrose showed how far ahead of the pack they are by achieving a clean sweep, winning the BT Premiership outright by a considerable margin, then triumphing in the play-offs

with a 16–13 result against Ayr before retaining the BT Cup title with a 45–12 victory over Stirling County at Murrayfield.

Melrose also had the BT Premiership player of the season in midfielder Craig Jackson, whose cousin Ruaridh is a Scotland international. The Melrose member of the family is an example of a player who was overlooked as a teenager and as a result slipped through the professional net.

At the other end of the BT Premiership, Marr's stay in the top flight lasted only one season, while under-threat Hawick, thanks to the mid-season recruitment of the former Scotland assistant coach and international prop George Graham, avoided relegation, as did Glasgow Hawks, who, frustrated by not being awarded a Super Six franchise vented their ire on Jed-Forest in the promotion play-off with a crushing defeat of the Border club. Meanwhile Edinburgh Accies, having won the national league, return to Premiership rugby.

Super Six will now make it hard for clubs like Currie, despite its fostering a number of under-20 Scotland representatives and Sevens caps and establishing a high-quality coaching system, to continue on an upward trajectory. Currie will almost certainly lose a number of top players, leading to the possibility of the Malleny Park club being left behind in a backwater of second-tier rugby.

The ramifications of Super Six are difficult to foresee but if it produces more players ready to step into the professional game then it will be judged a success. This elite pathway may be the answer for Scotland to keep up with the international pack but if the grassroots are not tended then the feeder system will suffer. And these plaudits heaped on Glasgow Warriors might become just a distant memory.

WALES: CHALENGING FOR HONOURS AGAIN

by DAVID STEWART

Trophies are being delivered and challenged for by the Blues and Scarlets; a commensurate improvement at the Ospreys and the Dragons would be very welcome.

Too many recent editions of *Wooden Spoon Rugby World* have regretted that Welsh teams were not challenging for honours in the Guinness Pro14, much less being a serious factor in the premier European competition. How pleasing then to record that the Scarlets mounted a sturdy defence of their title in reaching another play-off final in Dublin, and qualified for the semi-final of what we can once again call the Heineken Cup – beating better-resourced outfits in Toulon and La Rochelle en route. Add the triumph of Cardiff Blues at Bilbao in the European Challenge Cup, and followers of the Welsh scene can be quietly satisfied that the graph of success – after an uncomfortably lean period – is in the right direction.

Simon Easterby having laid the foundations of a turnaround before accepting Joe Schmidt's invitation in 2014 to become the Irish forwards coach, Wayne Pivac – notably supported by Stephen Jones and Byron Hayward – has piloted Scarlets to their strongest position since regional rugby was introduced. Their early league form was extraordinary. Never out of the top two in their Pro14 Conference, the Scarlets only lost one game – 27–20 at Ulster – before the New Year.

Their good form led to so many players being called up by Warren Gatland for the Six Nations that the denuded squad occasionally struggled thereafter, including a surprising loss in Italy to the improving Benetton by 22–12 in February, and – in the absence of those being rested for the European semi-final at Leinster – a disappointing April trouncing at Edinburgh (52–14)

Unfortunately, the Irish province proved to be a nemesis for the Scarlets. A 38–16 defeat in that April semi-final had something of an 'action replay' when in the last game of the season, they went down again in Dublin (40–32). Perhaps translating league form into the European arena was the most notable achievement of Pivac – who as expected will become national coach after the 2019 World Cup – yet that required a significant turnaround in their pool.

The opening game in Toulon saw a frustrating single point defeat (21–20), but going down at home to Bath a week later (13–18) was a major disappointment. Back-to-back wins against Benetton in December paved the way for a season-defining victory at the Rec, 17–35; the opening try that night from a side-stepping Tadgh Beirne will live long in the memories of those who saw it. Likewise, a week later when thrice tournament winners Toulon were dispatched 30–27; most of the 14,500 at Parc y Scarlets saw the new stadium finally recapture the emotional tidal wave for which its Stradey predecessor was famed.

The La Rochelle quarter-final in late March was another afternoon when it felt like the good old days were back – 'the place was bouncing' pronounced WRU Chairman Gareth Davies, who hails from nearby Tumble. The capacity crowd, stretching to more than 15,300 this time, saw the much fancied French team vanquished 29–17.

Beirne had a remarkable season, starting 29 games; for context, Rhys Patchell was next on 22. Beirne's heavy load was largely due to Jake Ball managing only six appearances because of injury. The wonderfully consistent performances of the Leinster academy product were rewarded with his first international caps in Australia. He heads to Munster with the thanks and good wishes of his team-mates and supporters.

The cutting edge provided by full back/wing Johnny McNicholl raised hopes that the Cantabrian will avail himself of the three-year residency rule to become available for Wales. Regrettably, the success of Hadleigh Parkes in that regard means Scott Williams is transferring a dozen miles east to the Ospreys. Another departure, to Edinburgh, is the much admired John Barclay; he came to West Wales seeking to revitalise his career, and left it as Scotland's captain.

The leadership of British Lions hooker Ken Owens was key, the progress of his deputy Ryan Elias hugely encouraging, as was the rehabilitation of Samson Lee following a difficult injury for a tight-head prop, while on the other side Rob Evans progressed to world class. With David Bulbring and Lewis Rawlins supplying the heft alongside Beirne in support of their front-row colleagues, the Scarlets had a sound base for playing the fluid and thinking football (echoes of Carwyn James), which provided so much of their success – fundamental to this was the handling skill and decision-making of their tight forwards.

Behind them, flankers Aaron Shingler and James 'Cubby' Davies had breakthrough seasons. The former, once a promising opening bowler at Glamorgan, had the misfortune to suffer a nasty knee injury in the Pro14 final, so will be eager to renew his challenge for a World Cup place once fit again; the latter – a character to follow the likes of Ray Gravelle – having originally been known as an Olympic Sevens player, is now making an irresistible claim to be part of Gatland's run-on XV selection.

The Scarlets will quietly fancy Europe in the new season, being top seeds in a pool with Racing 92, Leicester and Ulster. Similarly, the Blues will not be intimidated by a Heineken draw which puts them with Saracens, Glasgow and Lyon.

A year ago, we noted steady progress by the Blues, who won 50 per cent of their league matches. This year's 11 wins from 21 in Conference 'A' – 54 points, a fourth-place finish – hints at a status quo in terms of bread-and-butter performances. Closer examination reveals a poor start, defeats at home to Edinburgh (10–20) and Glasgow (19–20), and away to Leinster (37–9) and Munster (39–16) made for an unhappy September. Europe kick-started their season, with a win at Toulouse (15–17) in the first round of matches. They went on to do the double over the former European champions, as well as winning home and away against Lyon, and at home to Sale – a highly creditable five wins out of six, which led to their winning run in the European Challenge Cup – covered in depth elsewhere in this year's Annual.

Off the field, there are significant changes. Long-standing chairman and funder Peter Thomas is standing down; older readers may recall he hooked for Cardiff

LEFT Tadgh Beirne of Scarlets goes over for his side's third try during the European Champions Cup match in Llanelli between Scarlets and Benetton on 9 December 2017.

Rags (2nd XV in the amateur era). On the playing side, highly regarded coach Danny Wilson signalled in mid-season he would not seek a renewal of his contract. No sooner had he arranged to work under former Blues coach Dai Young at Wasps, than Gregor Townsend came calling – the Scotland forwards coach Dan McFarland, having agreed to take charge at Ulster. A lengthy search for Wilson's replacement resulted in the appointment of Australian John Mulvihill, previously at Western Force and in Japan – meaning that none of the Welsh regions is now led by a local coach.

Ospreys have also had a change at the helm. A shockingly poor start to the season brought a mere three Pro14 wins by Christmas. Ironically, they raised their form in the European Champions Cup running the powerful Clermont Auvergne (21–26) and Saracens (36–34) close in October and winning back-to-back against fellow strugglers Northampton Saints in December (32–43 and 32–15). It was not enough to keep Steve Tandy in post after six seasons. Former Ulster hooker Allen Clarke moved up from the forwards coach role on an interim basis in January, before being confirmed as the new head coach in April. They managed to win five of their last eight league games, including the notable 32–18 scalp of Leinster – resting those who had helped Ireland to the Grand Slam a week earlier – but it still meant a lowly fifth place in Conference 'A' on 44 points (by way of context, winners Glasgow finished with 76).

Player-wise, while Rhys Webb has left for Toulon with Dan Biggar going to Northampton, happily George North comes the other way. Aled Davies, another transfer from the Scarlets, should prove a lively presence at the base of the scrum with the talented Sam Davies outside him.

An end of season defeat at Ulster in a play-off for the last Heineken Cup place (3rd placed Cheetahs being ineligible) means Ospreys will play in the second-tier competition next term, their pool containing Worcester, Pau, and the rebuilding Stade Français. The Dragons, perpetual Challenge Cup participants for longer than they are comfortable with, are drawn with Timisoara from Romania, Northampton and Clermont.

A season that started with promise for the east Wales region turned into one of disappointment, new coach Bernard Jackman making clear his dissatisfaction with some of the playing staff. It seemed a curious approach to motivation of the sides he was putting out on a week by week basis. Placed sixth out of seven teams in Conference 'B', they enjoyed a mere two wins in early-season September against Connacht (21–8) and Southern Kings (29–13). Particularly disturbing were the margins of some defeats, notably in Ireland: Ulster 52–25, Munster 49–6, Leinster 54–10.

Their last victory was as early as 2 February in an Anglo-Welsh Cup clash with Worcester (33–27); the final seven matches of the season all ended in defeat, including at the hands of the Kings, Zebre and Treviso twice. And yet individual players still broke through to international honours: Cory Hill graduated to co-captaincy of the summer tour to the Americas, where Elliot Dee impressed, and Hallam Amos looked ready to join Hill as a regular in the Welsh side. Add Richard Hibbard and Ross Moriarty, Ryan Bevington and Rhodri Jones (lots of Rs!) repatriating from England, and the playing roster does appear stronger.

LEFT Ospreys' Alun Wyn Jones is tackled by Cardiff Blues' Garyn Smith during the Pro14 match on 28 April 2018 in Cardiff, won 26–23 by Ospreys. Jones scored the first try of the match.

BELOW Jeff Hassler of Ospreys in action against Luke Marshall of Ulster in the Pro14 play-off for the final Champions Cup place for 2018–19. Ulster won 35–17.

In terms of the wider picture, the regional scene appears in better health than for some years. Under the chairmanship of Gareth Davies, relationships with the union are much better, and good young players are being produced – as illustrated by those representing the national side in New York and Argentina. Crucially, trophies are being delivered and challenged for – this time by the Blues and Scarlets; a commensurate improvement at the Ospreys and the Dragons would be very welcome.

IRELAND: LANSDOWNE'S UNFORGETTABLE SEASON

by RUAIDHRI O'CONNOR

'We're the first Dublin club to win the All-Ireland League three times. When you consider we only got promoted back to this division in 2010–11, that's a good effort in seven, eight years. I'm really pleased with that.'

Mike Ruddock will always be widely known as the man who led Wales to their watershed Grand Slam in 2005 but in one corner of south Dublin he is building another legacy. Lansdowne have been a leading light in the Irish domestic game for a number of years now, but they have never enjoyed a campaign like the one just past when they swept all before them. A Leinster Senior Cup success led to the All Ireland Bateman Cup title, while their consistent form saw them top the Ulster Bank Division 1A table and they went on to justify their seeding by lifting the trophy outright. Play-off victories over Garryowen and Cork Constitution secured a third title in six seasons for the club who operate under the shadows of the Aviva Stadium in Ballsbridge.

Led by the experienced former Munster player Scott Deasy, who finished as the league's top scorer, and captain Ian Prendiville, their combination of experienced campaigners and young, ambitious players was a potent blend. With the calm head of former Leinster, Worcester Warriors and Wales coach Ruddock at the helm, they have enjoyed their most glorious period in recent times.

Since Shannon's long-established stranglehold on the division came to an end in 2009, this has been the league's most open decade. Five different clubs have won titles since the Limerick side last won the trophy and

this third title edges Lansdowne ahead of their rivals Con and Clontarf as the most successful club of the past decade.

Ruddock cut a contented figure at the end of it all as he reflected on his team's success. 'The All-Ireland League and Bateman Cup are tough competitions,' the 59-year-old said. 'Former Ireland coaches Eddie O'Sullivan, and, until he joined London Irish recently, Declan Kidney were both coaching in it this season. We won the League twice if you like, the regular season and the knock-out rounds, so are delighted with what we have achieved.

'Club rugby is demanding with a lot of hungry young players from the provinces pushing to further their careers. You're always improving and it's taken me 30-plus years to get to where I am now. You're constantly learning, but even though the game has changed, the fundamental principles of it are still there. You have to do the basics, line-out and scrummaging, well. Just look at the All Blacks – the foundations of their game are so strong, which creates the platform for their skills and dazzling running to come to the fore.'

Having won the league and Cup double themselves a year previously, Cork Constitution got themselves back into a position to retain both crowns but found the Dubliners too strong on both occasions.

Lansdowne, who finished 10 points ahead of a resurgent Terenure College in the league at the end of the 18-game regular season, were too good for Garryowen in the semi-final. With Adam Leavy – an Ireland Sevens international and younger brother of Grand Slam star Dan – crossing for a pair of tries, they proved far too strong, beating the former champions 36–19 on their return to the play-offs for the first time since 2009.

Despite ceding home advantage to Terenure for their semi-final, Con held few fears of travelling to the capital and, guided by fly half Tomas Quinlan – the star of last year's final – came away with a 22–15 win at Lakelands that set up a repeat of the Bateman Cup decider.

That had been a comprehensive 32–12 win in April, but things were a lot tighter at the Aviva Stadium a month later in the league final. The Dubliners needed a strong showing from their Leinster prop Peter Dooley whose scrummaging work caused all sorts of problems, while his big carry led to Tyrone Moran's all-important 61st minute try which was crucially converted by Deasy. Quinlan missed a penalty to win it as Con came on strong in the end-game, but Lansdowne survived to claim a 19–17 victory.

'Scott [Deasy] has been doing it for years, but in fairness he'll be the first to tell you that you can only do it if you're getting the forwards to give you the little bit of ball that you need to dictate matters, and to apply pressure,' Ruddock said of the final performance. 'The boys fronted up well. The boys behind (in the outside backs) didn't get too many chances, but they just made the tackles and that's important to us.'

'We're the first Dublin club to win the All-Ireland League three times. When you consider we only got promoted back to this division in 2010–11, that's a good effort in seven, eight years. I'm really pleased with that.'

So Lansdowne could celebrate another successful season while the league is set for another summer of change as the Irish Rugby Football Union (IRFU) contemplate life after the now defunct British and Irish Cup. The cross-border competition, designed to give game-time to budding professionals, was never popular with the clubs, and while there will be a tournament between the provinces and the Welsh regions next season it will be confined to the first weeks of the season. That should mean the clubs will have greater access to the best young professionals not being used by their provinces, which should improve the standards of, and interest in, the league.

RIGHT Lansdowne's Scott Deasy receives the man of the match award after guiding his team to victory in the Ulster Bank League final.

BELOW LEFT Lansdowne's Ian Prendiville is tackled by Joe McSwiney and Conor Kindregan of Cork Constitution during the League final.

There is speculation that the divisions could be re-aligned once again to ensure competitiveness, and the union are keen to engage the clubs themselves to ensure they are part of the decision-making process. 'There's still a bit of work to be done in that space,' IRFU performance director David Nucifora said in June. 'If we can take the alignment that we've got already in the game down another level then I think it would give us a significant advantage over our rivals.

'Because that's an area that around the world unions struggle with, building the bridge between the amateur game and the professional game. We've got to be careful that that gap doesn't open into a chasm because that wouldn't be good for the game. We've got to keep them as close together as we can. Hopefully what we put on the table here will be of benefit to everyone, not just the professional game but to the benefit of the club game as well.'

That should be music to the ears to those involved in the club game who have long felt somewhat ignored by those in the corridors of power.

Yet, the club game continues to play a role in Ireland's success and has acted as a gateway for those who struggle to make the breakthrough in the academy structure and need a little longer to make the step up to the professional game. Recently capped Scarlets star Tadhg Beirne, who has now moved to Munster, is an example of a player who struggled to get a look-in at Leinster but was scouted while playing for Ruddock's Lansdowne and featured in their last final outing.

Those structural changes won't be in place immediately, however, which means the top flight will be a Munster/Leinster carve-up in 2018–19 after Buccaneers went down as the league's bottom side.

The league's most successful club, Shannon, return to the top flight after a five-year absence. Coached by former Exeter Chiefs star Tom Hayes, they were pushed all the way by Banbridge but a final day win over University College Cork clinched top spot in Division 1B. However, the Cork students dusted themselves off for the play-offs and beat St Mary's and Banbridge away to reach the top flight for the first time, meaning it will be a 50/50 split between Leinster and Munster clubs. The news was not good for their fellow Leesiders, and long-time 1A stalwarts Dolphin, who were relegated from Division 1B with a paltry 15 points, with Division 2A champions Malone and play-off winners City of Armagh bolstering Ulster's numbers in the second tier.

Old Crescent claimed Division 2B, while Sligo won Division 2C as famous Dublin club Bective Rangers of Donnybrook joined neighbours Wanderers in dropping out of senior rugby after finishing bottom of the lowest league. They will be replaced by Mayo club Ballina, who last played on the national stage in 2005. The replacing of one of the game's traditional power-houses with a provincial side reflects the continuing demographic changes at the heart of Irish rugby.

The Ulster Bank League remains competitive, the standard at the top level is high and the players are committed to the cause but it seems the IRFU are determined to shake it up once more. The sparse attendance at the Aviva Stadium for the league final shows that there is work to do in finding a place for the league in the otherwise hugely successful Irish game.

Not that Lansdowne will care too much as they savour their bulging trophy cabinet after an unforgettable season.

FRANCE: A VICTORY FOR THE UNDERDOGS

by **CHRIS THAU**

'It will take a long time to get France back to where we want it to be. We must change the system from the amateur level upwards. We need a strong vision and everyone must be behind it.'

In France, the Top 14 regular season ended with the Montpellier club, owned by Mohed Altrad and coached by New Zealander Vern Cotter, at the top of the table with 81 championship points followed by last year's champions Racing with 80, Toulouse in third place with 74, Toulon fourth with 73, and Lyon fifth with 70. Castres Olympique, coached by 52-year old Christophe Urios a former club hooker, finished sixth with 69 points, having overtaken last year's finalists La Rochelle (67 points) in the final stages of the regular season. In the play-offs all hell broke loose with Castres, inspired by Urios, knocking out in succession Toulouse and Racing to reach the final showdown with the Montpellier juggernaut, a match played in front of 78,442 spectators at the Stade de France in Paris.

The unheralded Castres, made underdogs by both pundits and bookies, upset the form book by winning 29–13 (tries by Dumora and Mafi, converted by Urdapilleta, who added five more penalties for a 100 per cent match record of 19 points). It was a stupendous match, and a result that left both Montpellier coach Cotter and club owner Altrad speechless. This was Urios' second Bouclier de Brennus of the five won by Castres in their history, the coach having hooked for the team that won the title back in 1993. He has become one of France's hottest coaching properties, having won the respect of the inquisitive French media with his pre-match

statement 'We are ready for it.' He expanded on what he meant after the fast and furious match, which forced the star-studded Montpelier to run out of options.

'We make sure that we challenge the opposition on their strongest points, be it scrummaging, line out, or tackling. This is how our players prepare for this kind of encounter. We make sure to work hard, that the guys are under pressure all the time, especially during the training sessions on Tuesdays. We want the training to be much harder than the match, without the actual physical contact. To give you an example we only missed four out of the 143 tackles. Our main kickers, Ben Urdapilletta, Rory Kockott and Julien Dumora, were prepared for this kind of game and they performed to perfection. We worked for that, it was part of our game plan.'

According to his former 1993 teammate Adrian Lungu, nowadays also working for the Castres club, the secret of Urios is his uncanny ability to make the players want to work hard in training as if their lives depend on it, and also cunning man-management that helps weld the squad around his project as a genuine rugby family. 'Everyone is on the same page, starting with his coaching team, Frederic Charrier and Joe El Abd, both former captains of the Oyonnax club, which he coached a few years ago, and who have followed him to Castres, where they operate as a technical triumvirate,' said Lungu The appointment of Urios as coach of the French Barbarians (officially nominated by the FFR as France's national 2nd XV) for their tour to New Zealand in June, suggests that his performance is closely monitored by the French Federation, and is possibly a first step towards the top coaching job in France.

This is indeed a hot issue, given the circumstances of the dismissal of France coach Guy Novès, at the end of the previous year. The sacking of Novès, probably the most decorated French coach, after less than two years in the job, including the subsequent allegations of inappropriate conduct levelled by the FFR, did not go down well with the French rugby community. Regardless of the events, one cannot escape the feeling that Novès, like his predecessor Philippe Saint-André, had become a convenient, high-profile scapegoat for the deep-seated structural problems affecting French rugby, which the FFR officials like to talk about *ad nauseam*, but are unwilling, or perhaps unable, to solve. Unlike Novès' predecessor Philippe Saint-André, who was allowed by the then FFR President Pierre Camu to finish his term in office after the end of RWC 2015, the former Toulouse supremo was kicked out by the new President Bernard Laporte, before he could demonstrate whether his

BELOW LEFT Montpellier players look dejected as referee Jérôme Garcès awards a Castres try during the Top 14 final.

BELOW Rory Kockott of Castres puts up a box kick during the Top 14 final at the Stade de France, 2 June 2018.

LEFT Castres' head coach Christophe Urios looks pensive but determined before the Top 14 final with Castres.

BELOW LEFT Former All Black Conrad Smith of Pau in action against La Rochelle in March 2018; whether high-profile foreigners, however talented like Smith, benefit the French game is much in doubt.

RIGHT France captain Guilhem Guirado of Toulon seen during the Top 14 play-off match against Lyon at Felix Mayol Stadium, Toulon, 18 May 2018. The match finished 19–19 after extra time; Lyon won on tries scored.

methods might eventually work and France could make a positive impact at RWC 2019. In this respect, Novès' frustration is understandable, given his achievements and acknowledged expertise.

It is true his track record in charge of the French team was pretty dismal (seven wins out of the 21 matches, as well as a 23–23 draw with Japan at the end of November 2017) but he was brought in to rebuild the French team for 2019, not to win the Six Nations or a Test series in South Africa. Bernard Laporte, the 13th FRR President, who had successfully led the French bid for the 2023 RWC, did little to hide his disappointment, but has chosen a novel way to deal with Novès and his coaching team. Rather than sack him straight away, Laporte, himself a former coach of France and sports minister under President Nicolas Sarkozy, appointed his former teammate and long-term ally Serge Simon, now an FFR vice-president, to chair a commission, supposedly formed to examine what should be done to enable France to recapture the missing edge at the top of world rugby. It was quite disingenuous of Simon to claim that his inquiry had nothing to do with Novès, so unsurprisingly the media understood quickly that it was all a fudge. Nobody was surprised, then, that the outcome of the inquiry was to sack Novès, though both the timing and the manner of it shocked French rugby.

As former coach of the French team in both RWC 2003 and RWC 2007, and more recently of the Toulon club, Laporte is well-acquainted with the underlying problems besetting French rugby: the large number of foreign players flooding the French leagues, from Top 14 to Federale 3, is perceived as the main cause of the decline. Consequently the number of quality French players available for selection has been dwindling fast, with a corresponding decline in performance of the senior side. This is the underlying cause of the perennial substandard performances of *Les Bleus* during the last few years. Also important is a certain *laissez-faire* life-style, still prevailing among the elite French players.

Not that the French team under the newly appointed coach Jacques Brunel, himself a former assistant of Bernard Laporte, has set the world alight with its results since the sacking of Novès, though one could detect a greater sense of urgency among the selected players. Under Novès, France won two and lost three in the 2016 Six Nations and won three and lost two in 2017, a similar record to that achieved by Brunel's team in 2018. Under Novès, France lost all three Tests in South Africa in the summer of 2017, the same outcome as achieved by Brunel's team in New Zealand in 2018. Furthermore, if one examines the lists of players used by the two coaches, the differences are not particularly striking.

After the dismissal of Novès, the warning of former French international flanker Olivier Magne, that French rugby was in a long-term crisis made the headlines. The flanker, who made 89 appearances for France between 1997 and 2007, knows what he is talking about. He knows French rugby inside out, having commenced his playing career in Aurillac in 1979, followed by stints with Dax, Brive, Montferrand and eventually London Irish, not to mention his family connections with one of the best known rugby clans in the south-west of France, which includes father-in-law, Claude Dourthe, one of the finest centres in French rugby in the 1960s and a French selector and FFR official, and his brothers-in-law Richard Dourthe and Raphael Ibanez. 'It will take a long time to get France back to where we want it to be. We must change the system from the amateur level upwards. We need a strong vision and everyone must be behind it,' said Magne.

In other words, Novès is not the cause of the problems. So why then had Laporte chosen to summarily dismiss Novès and his team of Yannick Bru, J.-F. Dubois and Gerald Bastide, without warning. Even the owner of the Montpellier club Mohed Altrad, who is one of Laporte's backers and a sponsor of the French team, was critical of the way the FFR dealt with the former Toulouse supremo: 'I told him [Serge Simon] that the big issue with this French team is that it has got used to losing matches and to believe that the coaching is the problem would be a serious mistake . . . Novès did not deserve to be treated like that,' Altrad was quoted as saying.

The silver lining to an otherwise lacklustre international season was the win against Eddie Jones' England in the Six Nations as well as the outstanding performance of the French Under 20 team, which managed not only to defeat New Zealand (16–7) on its way to the final of the 2018 World Championship, but also demolish the seemingly unbeatable England 33–25 to win their first ever U20 gold medal.. It was sweet revenge for their Six Nations 22–6 defeat at the hands of the same U20 English side a few months earlier, which at the time drew the ire of the FFR top brass, who identified the age-group structure of French rugby as one of causes of the hardship experienced by the first team. The young French players begged to differ and showed not only that there was talent galore in French rugby, but also that the quality work of the French U20 coaching duo David Darricarrère and Eric Dasalmartini, helped by manager Sébastien Piqueronies, himself a former coach of the team, was indisputable and made the difference against very strong opponents. The reaction of the talented French U20 scrum half and captain Arthur Coville was quite revealing in this respect. 'This is to show those who claim that the development work in French rugby is not up to standard at the moment, that they are wrong,' he said.

ITALY: RESTRUCTURING THROUGHOUT

by **CHRIS THAU**

'I want this Italian team to be the best this country has ever produced. I want to change the whole system here and leave a lasting legacy ... if we keep on improving you never know where it will lead.'

The Italian international season started with a 21–19 win against Fiji in Catania on 11 November 2017 – the first of ten international matches played by the Italians in 2017–18. The season ended seven months later, with the Italy concluding the summer tour of Japan with a hard-fought 25–22 win, in the second of two Tests, at Kobe, the birthplace of Japanese rugby, on 16 June. (The team captained by hooker Leonardo Ghiraldini lost the first Test 34–17 after an eminently forgettable game in Oita.) Sandwiched in between the two wins there were eight consecutive defeats, which although varied in size, circumstances and impact, had one common factor – the inability of Italian rugby to convert its sizeable gains in terms of quality and talent into winning performances. Whether this is just a mental bloc, a question of resilience, or fitness, or a combination of these three, is the key to the Italian rugby conundrum which head coach Conor O'Shea is trying to solve. And although, statistically, this was just another unsuccessful season for O'Shea and the Italians, there is no doubt that statistics alone do not tell the full story.

The Irishman has embarked on a wide-ranging programme to change the flagging structure of Italian rugby, which not only does not match its ambitions but is also below the standard needed in the elite professional game. According to O'Shea's friend and mentor, former England coach Clive Woodward, this comprehensive approach is unlikely to succeed, because it prevents the one-time Ireland full back dedicating himself solely and completely to the coaching job. But O'Shea is painfully aware that in order to eliminate the historic fault lines preventing Italian rugby from fulfilling its potential, he must do both jobs, coaching and development, because in Italy's case one is not possible without the other. O'Shea's vision and ambitions have been made clear in an in-depth interview published in his native Ireland. 'I want this Italian team to be the best this country has ever produced. I want to change the whole system here and leave a lasting legacy. And I want that very badly because I'm driven, and I am ambitious and I want to be successful. But success can mean different things so we want to keep on improving, and if we keep on improving you never know where it will lead. We've a young team here, and I'd like to think they could be around for six or seven years,' he said.

O'Shea regards the prosperity of the two Italian professional franchises, Benetton and Zebre, as a crucial component of his remit and the one and only way to enable Italy to fulfil its potential. For Italy to start firing on all cylinders, Benetton and Zebre must do well. This is why he has involved himself heavily in the recruitment of the coaching staff for both teams, a first for an Italy head coach. This is how the former Irish skipper and Georgia assistant coach Michael Bradley has become the Zebre head coach, while former New Zealand full back and Canada coach Kieran Crowley has taken over at Benetton. With two world-class coaches working in tandem with the O'Shea's team, the playing style and the fortunes of the two franchises have changed beyond recognition. This season Benetton won a record eight matches in Pro14, while Zebre, the eternal whipping boys of European club rugby, won four matches and could have won twice as many. The Irishman is confident that sooner rather than later all these changes will reach critical mass and eventually impact the fortunes of the senior side, coached by himself and his team of Mike Catt, Brendan Venter and Wayne Smith, not to mention the unsung heroes of the O'Shea revolution, his old buddy Stephen Aboud, a former IRFU Technical Director who is now in charge of development, and the

RIGHT Fiji's Leone Nakarawa (left) and Italy's Sergio Parisse contest a line out during the November 2017 Test in Catania.

U20s, and Performance Director Peter Atkinson, a former Saracens and England Institute of Sport strength and conditioning coach. In fact, Italy's final match in the 2018 Six Nations, an unlucky 29–27 loss to Scotland in the closing stages of a thoroughly entertaining game, could be a sample of the things to come. The shift is unlikely to take place this year, but the second half of 2019 might just be the time when the new-look Italy will start to make its mark. A RWC quarter-final for the first time would be a sweet revenge for the indignities suffered since Italy joined the Six Nations at the turn of the century and would certify O'Shea's achievements, though it's a big ask to qualify from a pool including the All

Blacks and Springboks. The upheaval triggered off by the O'Shea revolution has now reached the lower tiers of the Italian game, comprising the amateur and semi-professional leagues, which provide the selectors of the development squad *Italia Emergenti* (Emerging Italy) as well as the U20 team and the two professional franchises with a steady stream of talent mainly from within the ranks of the leading clubs of the 10-club Eccellenza premiership, the likes of Padua, Calvisano, Rovigo and Fiamme Oro.

The regular season, the 88th of the premiership, ended with Petrarca Padova, coached by former Italian utility back Andrea Marcato, topping the table with 74 championship points (16 wins out of 18 matches), followed by Patarò Calvisano with 70 points, Femi CZ Rovigo 67 and Fiamme Oro 53, while the 2013 Champions Mogliano finished bottom of the table and were relegated to the second division In the home and away semi-finals Padova dismissed Fiamme Oro by an aggregate score of 60–27, while Calvisano scrambled through thanks to a one point difference (33–32) aggregate score against Rovigo. The 35-year old Marcato, whose drop goal in the closing stages of the 2008 Six Nations game against Scotland helped Italy, coached at the time by Nick Mallett, achieve a famous 23–20 win, then briefly became a celebrity, a status that did not last long as he got injured and dropped out of the international squad only a year later.

A championship final is not something that is belittled in the rugby-mad Veneto region and the young coach, himself a former Padova player, made a valid point in his pre-match assessment, saying that the event is big enough to concentrate the minds of his players. Indeed, his words sounded like an excerpt from one of O'Shea's speeches, a clear sign that the good work of the Irishman is spreading far and fast. 'The excitement of playing the final on our home ground "El Plebiscito" is enough for us. The build-up to this game works by itself. There is no need for additional motivation, or stirring speeches or anything else. For this game, more than ever, our focus will be on maintaining possession, defence and discipline. I really hope Saturday will be a great party, for Italian rugby, for the city of Padua and for all the Petrarca supporters,' Marcato said.

LEFT The diminutive Matteo Minozzi meets a high tackle during Italy's first 2018 summer Test with Japan.

BELOW LEFT George Biagi of Zebre is named as man of the match after his team's 19–11 victory in Connacht in February.

BELOW Petrarca centre Joaquin Andres Riera hunts for a gap in the Calvisano defence during his team's victory in the final.

And indeed, so it was! Seven long years after their previous success in the Championship (Scudetto) final, Petrarca Padova, defeated the holders Patarò Calvisano, 19–11, to secure the top trophy for the 13th time in the club's illustrious history. Like his coach a decade earlier it was Petrarca's outside half and man of the match, Andrea Menitti-Ippolito, who sealed the win with another drop goal, his second of the day, taking the sting out of Calvisano's determined fight-back.

A Summary of the Season 2017–18

by TERRY COOPER

INTERNATIONAL RUGBY

ARGENTINA TO EUROPE, NOVEMBER 2017

England	21	Argentina	8
Italy	15	Argentina	31
Ireland	28	Argentina	19

AUSTRALIA TO JAPAN & EUROPE, NOVEMBER 2017

Japan	30	Australia	63
Wales	21	Australia	29
England	30	Australia	6
Scotland	53	Australia	24

FIJI TO EUROPE, NOVEMBER 2017

Italy	19	Fiji	10
Ireland	23	Fiji	20

GEORGIA TO WALES, NOVEMBER 2017

Wales	13	Georgia	6

JAPAN TO EUROPE, NOVEMBER 2017

France	23	Japan	23

NEW ZEALAND TO EUROPE, NOVEMBER 2017

France	18	New Zealand	38
Scotland	17	New Zealand	22
Wales	18	New Zealand	33

SAMOA TO EUROPE, NOVEMBER 2017

Scotland	44	Samoa	38
England	48	Samoa	14

SOUTH AFRICA TO EUROPE, NOVEMBER 2017

Ireland	38	South Africa	3
France	17	South Africa	18
Italy	6	South Africa	35
Wales	24	South Africa	22

ENGLAND TO SOUTH AFRICA, JUNE 2018

South Africa	L	39–42
South Africa	L	12–23
South Africa	W	25–10
Played 3 Lost 2 Won 1		

WALES TO ARGENTINA, JUNE 2018

Argentina	W	23–10
Argentina	W	30–12
Played 2 Won 2		

SCOTLAND TO ARGENTINA, CANADA & USA, JUNE 2018

Argentina	W	44–15
Canada	W	48–10
USA	L	29–30
Played 3 Won 2 Lost 1		

IRELAND TO AUSTRALIA, JUNE 2018

Australia	L	9–18
Australia	W	26–21
Australia	W	20–16
Played 3 Won 2 Lost 1		

FRANCE TO NEW ZEALAND, JUNE 2018

New Zealand	L	11–52
New Zealand	L	13–26
NNew Zealand	L	14–49
Played 3 Lost 3		

ITALY TO JAPAN, JUNE 2018

Japan	L	17–34
Japan	W	25–22
Played 2 Lost 1 Won 1		

OTHER TIER 1 INTERNATIONAL MATCH

(Played in Washington, DC, June 2018)

Wales	22	South Africa	20

WORLD RUGBY PACIFIC NATIONS CUP 2018

(Played in Fiji, June 2018)

Tonga	15	Georgia	16
Fiji	24	Samoa	22
Tonga	28	Samoa	18
Fiji	37	Georgia	15

Winners: Fiji

RBS 6 NATIONS CHAMPIONSHIP 2018

Wales	34	Scotland	7
France	13	Ireland	15
Italy	15	England	46
Ireland	56	Italy	19
England	12	Wales	6
Scotland	32	France	26
France	34	Italy	17
Ireland	37	Wales	27
Scotland	25	England	13
Ireland	28	Scotland	8
France	22	England	16
Wales	38	Italy	14
Italy	27	Scotland	29
England	15	Ireland	24
Wales	14	France	13

	P	W	D	L	F	A	PD	TB	LB	Pts
Ireland	5	5	0	0	160	82	78	3	0	26
Wales	5	3	0	2	119	83	36	2	1	15
Scotland	5	3	0	2	101	128	-27	1	0	13
France	5	2	0	3	108	94	14	0	3	11
England	5	2	0	3	102	92	10	1	1	10
Italy	5	0	0	5	92	203	-111	0	1	1

WOMEN'S SIX NATIONS 2018

Wales	18	Scotland	17
France	24	Ireland	0
Italy	7	England	42
England	52	Wales	0
Scotland	3	France	26
Ireland	21	Italy	8
Scotland	8	England	43
France	57	Italy	0
Ireland	35	Wales	12
France	18	England	17
Wales	15	Italy	22
Ireland	12	Scotland	15
England	33	Ireland	11
Wales	3	France	38
Italy	26	Scotland	12

	P	W	D	L	F	A	PD	TB	LB	Pts
France	5	5	0	0	163	23	140	4	0	27
England	5	4	0	1	187	44	143	4	1	21
Ireland	5	2	0	3	79	92	13	1	1	10
Italy	5	2	0	3	63	147	-84	2	0	10
Scotland	5	1	0	4	55	125	-70	0	1	5
Wales	5	1	0	4	48	164	-116	0	1	5

UNDER 20 SIX NATIONS 2018

Italy	17	England	27
Wales	36	Scotland	3
France	34	Ireland	24
Ireland	38	Italy	34
England	37	Wales	12
Scotland	19	France	69
France	78	Italy	12
Ireland	38	Wales	41
Scotland	24	England	17
Ireland	30	Scotland	25
Wales	7	Italy	18
France	6	England	22
Italy	45	Scotland	31
England	48	Ireland	15
Wales	3	France	24

	P	W	D	L	F	A	PD	TB	LB	Pts
France	5	4	0	1	211	80	131	4	0	20
England	5	4	0	1	151	74	77	3	1	20
Ireland	5	2	0	3	145	182	-37	3	1	12
Italy	5	2	0	3	126	181	-55	2	1	11
Wales	5	2	0	3	99	120	-21	2	0	10
Scotland	5	1	0	4	102	197	-95	2	1	7

WORLD RUGBY UNDER-20 CHAMPIONSHIP

(Played in France)

Semi-finals

England	32	South Africa	31
New Zealand	7	France	16

Third-place play-off

South Africa	42	New Zealand	30

Final

England	25	France	33

RBS RUGBY EUROPE UNDER-18 CHAMPIONSHIP

(Played in Poland)

Third-place play-off

Spain	17	Portugal	0

Final

France	3	Georgia	8

BARBARIANS

Opponents	Result	
Classic Wallabies	W	27–24
Australia XV	L	28–31
NZ XV	L	22–31
Tonga	W	27–24
Munster	W	19–0
British Army	W	37–0
England XV	W	63–45

Played 7: W5 L2

THE RUGBY CHAMPIONSHIP 2017

Australia	34	New Zealand	54
(also 1st tie in Bledisloe Cup)			
South Africa	37	Argentina	15
New Zealand	35	Australia	29
(also 2nd tie in Bledisloe Cup)			
Argentina	23	South Africa	41
New Zealand	39	Argentina	22
Australia	23	South Africa	23
New Zealand	57	South Africa	0
Australia	45	Argentina	20
South Africa	27	Australia	27
Argentina	10	New Zealand	36
South Africa	24	New Zealand	25
Argentina	20	Australia	37

	P	W	L	D	PD	BP	Pts
New Zealand	6	6	0	0	127	4	28
Australia	6	2	2	2	-16	3	15
South Africa	6	2	2	2	-18	2	14
Argentina	6	0	6	0	-125	0	0

Champions: New Zealand

Bledisloe Cup
3rd Tie

Australia	23	New Zealand	18

Winners: New Zealand

2018 RUGBY EUROPE CHAMPIONSHIP

	P	W	D	L	F	A	TB	LB	GS	Pts
Georgia	5	5	0	0	188	35	3	0	1	24
Russia	5	2	0	3	142	84	2	1	0	11
Germany	5	0	0	5	34	359	0	0	0	0
Belgium*	5	2	0	3	106	182	1	0	0	-1
Spain*	5	3	0	2	146	74	1	0	0	-7
Romania*	5	3	0	2	198	80	2	0	0	-11

* Points deducted. Georgia and Russia qualify for RWC 2019. Germany join play-off process.
GS = Grand Slam bonus point.

SELECTED RWC 2019 QUALIFYING MATCHES

* Countries now qualified for RWC 2019
† Countries joining Repechage tournament

Asia play off

Cook Islands	3	Hong Kong†	26
Hong Kong†	51	Cook Islands	0

Europe play-off

Germany	16	Portugal	13

Europe/Oceania play-off

Samoa*	66	Germany†	15
Germany†	28	Samoa*	42

Americas play-off

Canada†	29	Uruguay*	38
Uruguay*	32	Canada†	31

Rugby Africa Gold Cup, 2018

	P	W	D	L	PD	Pts
Namibia*	5	5	0	0	278	25
Kenya†	5	4	0	1	71	17
Uganda	5	2	0	3	-12	9
Tunisia	5	2	0	3	-213	9
Zimbabwe	5	1	1	3	-23	8
Morocco	5	0	1	4	-98	3

Namibia* qualify for RWC2019 as Africa 1;
Kenya† join Repechage tournament.

HSBC WORLD RUGBY SEVENS SERIES FINALS 2017–18

Dubai

New Zealand	12	South Africa	24

South Africa (Cape Town)

New Zealand	38	Argentina	14

Australia (Sydney)

Australia	29	South Africa	0

New Zealand (Hamilton)

Fiji	24	South Africa	17

USA (Las Vegas)

USA	28	Argentina	0

Canada (Vancouver)

Fiji	31	Kenya	12

Hong Kong

Kenya	12	Fiji	24

Singapore

Fiji	28	Australia	22

England (Twickenham)

Fiji	21	South Africa	17

France (Paris)

South Africa	24	England	14

Champions: South Africa

HSBC WORLD RUGBY WOMEN'S SEVENS SERIES FINALS 2017–18

Dubai

USA	0	Australia	34

Australia (Sydney)

Australia	21	New Zealand	0

Japan (Kitakyushu)

New Zealand	24	France	12

Canada (Langford)

New Zealand	46	Australia	0

France (Paris)

New Zealand	33	Australia	7

Champions: Australia

CLUB, COUNTY AND DIVISIONAL RUGBY

ENGLAND

Aviva Premiership

	P	W	D	L	F	A	TB	LB	Pts
Exeter	22	17	0	5	618	354	13	4	85
Saracens	22	16	0	6	731	350	10	3	77
Wasps	22	14	1	7	615	501	10	3	71
Newcastle	22	14	0	8	455	506	7	0	63
Leicester	22	13	0	9	537	472	5	6	63
Bath	22	11	0	11	572	531	8	4	56
Gloucester	22	11	1	10	490	597	8	2	56
Sale	22	10	0	12	556	531	9	5	54
Northampton	22	8	0	14	509	645	5	6	43
Harlequins	22	7	0	15	479	640	5	3	36
Worcester	22	7	0	15	432	601	5	3	36
London Irish	22	3	0	19	385	651	3	7	22

Relegated: **Bristol**

Aviva Premiership Play-offs

Semi-finals

Exeter	36	Newcastle	5
Saracens	57	Wasps	33

Final

Exeter	10	Saracens	27

Greene King IPA RFU National Championship

	P	W	D	L	PD	Pts
Bristol	22	21	0	1	532	103
Ealing Trailfinders	22	16	1	5	244	83
Bedford Blues	22	11	2	9	78	68
Cornish Pirates	22	12	0	10	104	67
Jersey Reds	22	13	1	8	62	65
Yorkshire Carnegie	22	12	2	8	-29	63
Doncaster Knights	22	9	1	12	-33	57
Nottingham	22	10	1	11	-72	52
Richmond	22	9	0	13	-153	46
Hartpury College	22	6	1	15	-143	42
London Scottish	22	6	1	15	-186	40
Rotherham Titans	22	2	0	20	-404	14

Promoted to Premiership: Bristol

National Leagues

National 1 Champions: Coventry
Runners-up: Darlington Mowden Park
National 2 (S) Champions: Cinderford
National 2 (N) Champions: Sale

Play-off, National 2 N & S runners-up:
Chinnor	40	Sedgley Park	31

RFU Knockout Trophies Finals

Intermediate Cup
Camberley	63	Droitwich	14

Senior Vase
Wath Upon Dearne	22	Saltash	18

Junior Vase
Old Otliensians	32	South Molton	21

Tyrells Premier 15s League

	P	W	D	L	F	A	TB	LB	Pts
Saracens	18	15	1	2	648	193	15	2	79
Harlequins	18	15	0	3	674	289	14	2	76
Wasps	18	13	0	5	534	254	14	3	69
Glos.-Hartpury	18	11	1	6	572	380	14	0	60
Loughborough	18	10	1	7	383	368	9	2	53
Bristol Bears	18	9	0	9	481	343	8	2	46
Richmond	18	7	1	10	264	435	5	1	31
Darlington MP	18	4	1	13	284	413	5	3	26
Waterloo	18	2	2	14	223	495	1	3	16
Worcester	18	0	1	17	97	990	0	0	2

Tyrells Premier 15s Play-offs

First legs
Gloucester-Hartpury	0	Saracens Women	62
Wasps FC Ladies	19	Harlequins Ladies	25

Second legs
Saracens Women	45	Glos.-Hartpury	26
Harlequins Ladies	22	Wasps FC Ladies	7

Final
Saracens Women	24	Harlequins Ladies	20

County Championship Div. 1 Final (Bill Beaumont Cup)
Lancashire	32	Hertfordshire 16

County Championship Division 2 Final
Durham	46	Warwickshire 12

Jason Leonard National Under-20 Championship
Yorkshire	63	Cornwall	11

National Under-20 Division 2 Final
Lancashire	54	Notts, Lincs, Derby 38

BUCS Competitions:
Men's Championship Winners: Exeter
Women's Championship Winners: Exeter

Varsity Match
Men
Oxford	10	Cambridge	20
Women
Oxford	0	Cambridge	24

Inter-Services Championship:
Royal Navy	9	Royal Air Force	8
Royal Air Force	13	The Army	12
The Army	22	Royal Navy	14

Babcock Trophy Winners: The Army

Natwest Schools Cup Finals day
Under-18 Cup Winners: Warwick School
Under-18 Vase Winners: Langley School
Under-15 Cup Winners: Whitgift School
Under-15 Vase Winners: Beechen Cliff School

Natwest Schools Champion Trophy
Dulwich College

SCOTLAND

BT Premiership

	P	W	L	D	F	A	TB	LB	Pts
Melrose	18	16	2	0	579	285	12	2	78
Currie	18	15	3	0	598	229	13	1	74
Ayr	18	11	7	0	560	456	11	2	57
Watsonians	18	10	8	0	531	456	10	3	53
Heriot's	18	10	7	1	443	327	6	4	52
Boroughmuir	18	7	11	0	420	534	4	5	37
Stirling County	18	5	13	0	442	588	7	5	32
Hawick	18	6	12	0	372	481	3	3	30
Glasgow Hawks	18	5	12	1	364	565	5	3	30
Marr	18	4	14	0	371	619	5	2	23

BT Premiership Play-offs

Semi-finals

Melrose	37	Watsonians	8
Ayr	24	Currie	21

Final

Melrose	16	Ayr	13

BT National League Division 1

	P	W	L	D	F	A	TB	LB	Pts
Ed'burgh Acad.	22	21	1	6	976	246	20	0	104
Jed-Forest	22	21	1	0	898	432	20	0	104
GHA.	22	13	9	0	732	516	16	3	73
Dundee HSFP	22	12	10	0	617	463	14	6	68
Selkirk	22	13	9	0	641	480	11	2	65
Gala	22	11	10	1	548	538	10	4	60
Ab'deen Gram.	22	11	11	0	622	591	12	3	59
Kelso	22	9	12	1	539	654	10	3	51
Musselburgh	22	7	12	3	531	747	9	3	46
Cartha QP	22	7	15	0	514	661	9	5	42
Stewarts Mel.	22	3	19	0	371	788	6	8	24
Falkirk	22	3	19	0	371	788	6	6	24

BT Premiership-National 1 Play-off

Jed-Forest	0	Glasgow Hawks	46

BT National Cup Final

Melrose	45	Stirling County	12

BT Shield Final

Hawick	19	Carrick RFC	39

BT Bowl Final

Ross Sutherland	12	Wigtownshire	3

Scottish Sevens Winners

Kelso:	Melrose
Selkirk:	Selkirk
Melrose:	Watsonians
Hawick:	Watsonians
Berwick:	Watsonians
Langholm:	Watsonians
Peebles:	Watsonians
Gala:	Jed-Forest
Earlston:	Melrose
Jed-Forest:	Melrose
Kings of the Sevens:	Watsonians

BT Women's Premiership League

Winners: Hillhead Jordanhill

BT Women's Premiership National League 1

Winners: Annan

Sarah Beaney Cup Final

Winners: Hillhead Jordanhill

WALES

National Cup

Final

Merthyr	41	Newport	7

National Plate Final

Brynmawr	50	Nant Conwy	29

National Bowl Final

Porthcawl	33	Pembroke	31

Principality Premiership

	P	W	D	L	F	A	TB	LB	Pts
Merthyr	15	13	0	2	474	263	10	1	71
Llandovery	15	12	0	3	391	310	7	1	63
Pontypridd	15	12	0	3	457	327	7	0	62
RGC 1404	15	9	1	5	513	328	8	4	58
Carmarthen Q.	15	10	1	4	364	303	6	3	57
Ebbw Vale	15	10	0	5	327	237	3	3	48
Bedwas	15	8	0	7	413	348	6	4	48
Cardiff	15	7	0	8	394	352	6	4	43
Newport	15	7	0	8	366	381	6	5	43
Bridgend	15	8	0	7	319	336	2	2	39
Cross Keys	15	6	0	9	346	394	8	2	37
Aberavon	15	6	0	9	285	298	3	5	37
Llanelli	15	6	0	9	399	485	6	2	36
Swansea	15	2	0	13	255	472	1	5	16
Bargoed	15	2	0	13	231	484	3	1	13
Neath	15	1	0	14	277	493	2	5	12

National Championship

	P	W	D	L	F	A	TB	LB	Pts
Pontypool	22	22	0	0	926	239	19	0	107
Narberth	22	14	1	7	595	439	11	3	72
Trebanos	22	14	0	8	501	535	9	4	69
Tata Steel	22	13	0	9	546	483	10	4	66
Newbridge	22	12	0	10	460	461	7	3	58
Bedlinog	22	10	2	10	480	501	9	5	58
Rhydyfelin	22	10	0	12	391	435	4	5	49
N'castle Emlyn	22	9	1	12	470	633	6	3	47
Beddau	22	8	0	14	379	543	5	6	43
Cardiff Met.	22	7	2	13	473	638	5	3	40
Skewen	22	7	0	15	351	535	2	4	34
Glynneath	22	3	0	19	292	622	2	3	17

National League Champions

Division 1 East:	Brynmawr
Division 1 East Central:	Ystrad Rhonda
Division 1 West:	Felinfoel
Division 1 West Central:	Maesteg Harlequins
Division 1 North:	Nant Conwy
Division 2 East:	Hartridge
Division 2 East Central:	Gilfach Goch
Division 2 West:	Whitland
Division 2 West Central:	Maesteg Celtic
Division 2 North:	Denbigh

Women's Premier Division

Champions: Swansea

Women's Super Cup Final

Swansea	46	Caernarfon	18

IRELAND

Ulster Bank League Division 1A

	P	W	D	L	F	A	TB	LB	Pts
Lansdowne	18	16	0	2	515	273	7	0	71
Terenure Col.	18	12	0	6	456	333	10	3	61
Cork Con.	18	11	0	7	439	331	7	5	56
Garryowen.	18	12	0	6	445	362	6	2	56
Clontarf	18	11	0	7	435	386	9	2	55
Young Munster	18	9	0	9	397	355	6	6	48
UCD	18	6	0	12	376	406	6	7	37
Dublin Univ.	18	7	0	11	299	544	2	2	32
St Mary's Col.	18	4	0	14	279	480	1	4	21
Buccaneers	18	2	0	16	254	425	0	6	14

Ulster Bank League Division 1A Final
Lansdowne　　　　19　Cork Constitution　17

Ulster Bank League Division 1B

	P	W	D	L	F	A	TB	LB	Pts
Shannon	18	13	1	4	465	285	7	3	64
Banbridge	18	12	2	4	429	367	7	3	62
Ballynahinch	18	15	1	2	517	308	9	1	72
UCC	18	11	0	7	368	285	4	6	54
Old Belvedere	18	11	0	7	406	395	4	4	52
Naas	18	10	2	6	415	413	6	1	51
Ballymena	18	7	1	10	346	406	2	6	38
Old Wesley	18	7	0	11	367	429	6	3	37
U.L. Bohemians	18	6	1	11	303	363	3	7	36
Dolphin	18	8	0	10	293	380	1	1	34

Ulster Bank League Division 2A
Champions:　　　　Malone

Ulster Bank League Division 2B
Champions:　　　　Old Crescent

Ulster Bank League Division 2C
Champions:　　　　Navan

Ulster Bank All Ireland Bateman Cup Final
Cork Constitution　12　Lansdowne　32

All Ireland Junior Cup Final
Ashborne　　　　18　Kilfeacle & District　9

Fraser McMullen U-21 Cup
Dublin Univ.　　　41　Clontarf　　　21

All Ireland Women's League Div. 1
Champions:　　　　U.L. Bohemians

Women's All Ireland Cup
Railway Union　　33　U.L. Bohemians　3

Women's Inter-Provincial Series
Champions:　　　　Munster

ITALY

National Championship of Excellence
Semi-finals
Patarò Calvisano　24　Rovigo　　　　20
Petrarca Padova　24　Fiamme Oro Roma　10

Final
Petrarca Padova　19　Patarò Calvisano　11

FRANCE

Top 14

	P	W	D	L	F	A	TB	LB	Pts
Montpellier	26	17	0	9	752	559	11	2	81
Racing 92	26	18	0	8	622	478	5	3	80
Toulouse	26	16	1	9	719	595	4	4	74
Toulon	26	14	0	12	766	507	9	8	73
Lyon	26	15	0	11	689	545	7	3	70
Castres	26	15	0	11	638	624	4	5	69
La Rochelle	26	14	1	11	686	531	6	3	67
Pau	26	15	0	11	590	584	2	4	66
Clermont	26	11	1	14	629	687	4	4	54
Bordeaux	26	10	1	15	557	623	2	4	48
Agen	26	10	0	16	537	757	2	4	46
Stade Français	26	9	0	17	540	740	2	4	42
Oyonnax	26	7	3	16	566	824	1	4	39
Brive	26	7	1	18	485	726	1	5	36

Top 14 play-offs
Semi-finals
Castres Olympique　19　Racing Metro 92　14
Montpellier　　　　40　Lyon Rugby　14

Final
Montpellier　　　　13　Castres Olympique 29

GUINNESS PRO14

Conference 'A'

	P	W	D	L	F	A	TB	LB	Pts
Glasgow	21	15	1	5	614	366	12	2	76
Munster	21	13	1	7	568	361	10	5	69
Cheetahs	21	12	0	9	609	554	10	5	63
Cardiff Blues	21	11	0	10	502	482	5	5	54
Ospreys	21	9	0	12	390	487	5	3	44
Connacht	21	7	0	14	445	477	5	6	39
Zebre	21	7	0	14	408	593	4	4	36

Conference 'B'

	P	W	D	L	F	A	TB	LB	Pts
Leinster	21	14	1	6	601	374	10	2	70
Scarlets	21	14	1	6	528	365	9	3	70
Edinburgh	21	15	0	6	494	375	7	1	68
Ulster	21	12	2	7	538	482	8	2	62
Benetton	21	11	0	10	415	451	6	5	55
Dragons	21	2	2	17	378	672	4	4	20
Southern Kings	21	1	0	20	378	829	4	3	11

Play-offs
Quarter-finals
(played between teams ranked 2nd and 3rd in each of the two Conferences).

Scarlets　　　　43　Cheetahs　　　8
Munster　　　　20　Edinburgh　　16

Semi-finals
Glasgow Warriors　13　Scarlets　　　28
Leinster　　　　16　Munster　　　15

Final
Leinster　　　　40　Scarlets　　　32

THE BRITISH & IRISH CUP

Final
Ealing Trailfinders　22　Leinster A　　7

EUROPEAN RUGBY CHAMPIONS CUP

Pool 1

	P	W	D	L	F	A	TB	LB	Pts
La Rochelle	6	4	0	2	156	121	3	1	20
Wasps	6	3	0	3	154	121	4	1	17
Ulster	6	4	0	2	132	118	1	0	17
Harlequins	6	1	0	5	106	188	2	1	7

Pool 2

	P	W	D	L	F	A	TB	LB	Pts
Clermont	6	5	0	1	165	104	2	0	22
Saracens	6	3	1	2	205	146	3	1	18
Ospreys	6	2	1	3	152	148	3	2	15
Northampton	6	1	0	5	115	239	2	0	6

Pool 3

	P	W	D	L	F	A	TB	LB	Pts
Leinster	6	6	0	0	176	93	3	0	27
Exeter	6	3	0	3	138	117	1	2	15
Montpellier	6	2	0	4	130	163	3	2	13
Glasgow	6	1	0	5	128	199	2	1	7

Pool 4

	P	W	D	L	F	A	TB	LB	Pts
Munster	6	4	1	1	167	87	2	1	21
Racing 92	6	4	0	2	128	105	1	2	19
Castres	6	2	1	3	111	161	2	0	12
Leicester	6	1	0	5	118	171	1	2	7

Pool 5

	P	W	D	L	F	A	TB	LB	Pts
Scarlets	6	4	0	2	162	123	3	2	21
Toulon	6	4	0	2	159	125	1	2	19
Bath	6	4	0	2	151	121	1	1	18
Benetton	6	0	0	6	97	200	2	2	4

Quarter-finals

Scarlets	29	La Rochelle	17
Munster	20	Toulon	19
Clermont	17	Racing	28
Leinster	30	Saracens	19

Semi-finals

Leinster	38	Scarlets	16
Racing	27	Munster	22

Final

Leinster	15	Racing	12

AMLIN EUROPEAN CHALLENGE CUP

Quarter-finals

Newcastle	25	Brive	10
Pau	35	SF Paris	32
Connacht	28	Gloucester	33
Edinburgh	6	Cardiff	20

Semi-finals

Newcastle	12	Gloucester	33
Cardiff	16	Pau	10

Final

Gloucester	30	Cardiff	31

SUPER RUGBY TOURNAMENT 2018

	P	W	D	L	F	A	TB	LB	Pts
Crusaders	16	14	0	2	542	295	7	0	63
Lions	16	9	0	7	519	435	6	4	46
Waratahs	16	9	1	6	557	445	4	2	44
Hurricanes	16	11	0	5	474	343	5	2	51
Chiefs	16	11	0	5	463	368	3	2	49
Highlanders	16	10	0	6	437	445	3	1	44
Jaguares	16	9	0	7	409	418	2	0	38
Sharks	16	7	1	8	437	442	2	4	36
Rebels	16	7	0	9	440	461	5	3	36
Brumbies	16	7	0	9	393	422	2	4	34
Stormers	16	6	0	10	390	423	0	5	29
Bulls	16	6	0	10	441	502	2	3	29
Reds	16	6	0	10	389	501	1	3	28
Blues	16	4	0	12	378	509	2	4	22
Sunwolves	16	3	0	13	404	664	0	2	14

Quarter-finals

Hurricanes	32	Chiefs	31
Crusaders	40	Sharks	10
Waratahs	30	Highlanders	23
Lions	40	Jaguars	23

Semi-finals

Crusaders	30	Hurricanes	12
Lions	44	Waratahs	26

Final

Crusaders	37	Lions	18

SOUTH AFRICA

Currie Cup 2017

Final

Western Province	33	Sharks	21

NEW ZEALAND

Mitre 10 Cup 2017

Final

Canterbury	35	Tasman	13

Mitre 10 Premiership 2017

Winners: Canterbury

Mitre 10 Championship 2017

Winners: Wellington

Heartland Champions 2017

Meads Cup:	Wanganui
Lochore Cup:	Mid Canterbury

Ranfurly Shield

Holders :   Taranaki
(as of 4 Aug. 2018)

6

PREVIEW OF THE
SEASON 2018-19

Key Players

selected by IAN ROBERTSON

ENGLAND

JOE LAUNCHBURY
Wasps
Born: 12 April 1991
Height: 6ft 6in Weight: 19st 1lb
Lock – 54 caps, 20 points
1st cap v Fiji 2012

JONNY MAY
Leicester
Born: 1 April 1990
Height: 6ft 2in Weight: 14st 2lb
Winger – 37 caps, 85 points
1st cap v Argentina 2013

SCOTLAND

HUW JONES
Glasgow
Born: 17 December 1993
Height: 6ft 1in Weight: 15st 1lb
Centre – 16 caps, 50 points
1st cap v Japan 2016

JOHN BARCLAY
Edinburgh
Born: 24 September 1986
Height: 6ft 3in Weight: 16st 7lb
Back-row – 71 caps, 30 points
1st cap v New Zealand 2007

WALES

GARETH DAVIES
Scarlets
Born: 18 August 1990
Height: 5ft 10in Weight: 13st 12lb
Scrum half – 33 caps, 55 points
1st cap v South Africa 2014

ROSS MORIARTY
Gloucester
Born: 18 April 1994
Height: 6ft 2in Weight: 16st 3lb
Back-row – 23 caps, 10 points
1st cap v Ireland 2015

Six Nations Championship

2019

IRELAND

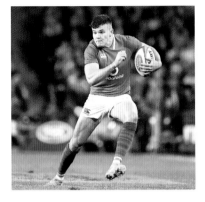

JACOB STOCKDALE
Ulster
Born: 3 April 1996
Height: 6ft 3in Weight: 16st 0lb
Winger – 11 caps, 55 points
1st cap v USA 2017

IAIN HENDERSON
Ulster
Born: 21 February 1992
Height: 6ft 7in Weight: 18st 5lb
Lock – 39 caps 25 points
1st cap v South Africa 2012

FRANCE

YACOUBA CAMARA
Toulouse
Born: 2 June 1994
Height: 6ft 5in Weight: 17st 0lb
Back-row – 11 caps
1st cap v Italy 2016

TEDDY THOMAS
Racing-Metro
Born: 18 September 1993
Height: 6ft 1in Weight: 14st 11lb
Winger – 13 caps, 40 points
1st cap v Fiji 2014

ITALY

MATTEO MINOZZI
Zebre
Born: 4 June 1996
Height: 5ft 9in Weight: 12st 10lb
Full back – 10 caps, 20 points
1st cap v Fiji 2017

ANDREA LOVOTTI
Zebre
Born: 28 July 1989
Height: 6ft 0in Weight: 17st 4lb
Prop – 27 caps
1st cap v France 2016

Fixtures 2018-19

AUGUST 2018

Sat 18   AUSTRALIA v NEW ZEALAND
(TRC & BC)
SOUTH AFRICA v ARGENTINA
(TRC)

Sat 25   NEW ZEALAND v AUSTRALIA
(TRC & BC)
ARGENTINA v SOUTH AFRICA
(TRC)

SEPTEMBER 2018

Fri Aug.31–   Gallagher English Premiership (1)
Sun 2 Sept   Greene King IPA Championship (1)
Fri Aug 31/   Guinness PRO14 (1)
Sat 1 Sept
Sat 1   English National Leagues
Tennent's Scottish Premiership (1)
Tennent's Scottish National
Leagues
Welsh Principality Premiership (1)
Welsh National Championship
Welsh National Leagues

Fri 7 & Sat 8   Guinness PRO14 (2)
Fri 7–Sun 9   Gallagher English Premiership (2)
Greene King IPA Championship (2)
Sat 8   NEW ZEALAND v ARGENTINA
(TRC)
AUSTRALIA v SOUTH AFRICA
(TRC)
English National Leagues
Tyrrells English Women's
Premier 15s
Tennent's Scottish Premiership (2)
Tennent's Scottish National
Leagues
Welsh Principality Premiership (2)
Welsh National Championship
Welsh National Leagues

Fri 14–Sun 16   Gallagher English Premiership (3)
Guinness PRO14 (3)
Greene King IPA Championship (3)
Sat 15   NEW ZEALAND v SOUTH AFRICA
(FC & TRC)
AUSTRALIA v ARGENTINA (TRC)
English National Leagues
Tyrrells English Women's
Premier 15s
Tennent's Scottish Premiership (3)
Tennent's Scottish National
Leagues
Welsh Principality Premiership (3)
Welsh National Championship
Welsh National Leagues

Fri 21–Sun 23   Gallagher England Premiership (4)
Greene King IPA Championship (4)

Fri 21/Sat 22   Guinness PRO14 (4)
Tyrrells English Women's
Premier 15s
Sat 22   English National Leagues
Tennent's Scottish Premiership (4)
Tennent's Scottish National
Leagues
Welsh Principality Premiership (4)
Welsh National Championship
Welsh National Leagues

Fri 28/Sat 29   Guinness PRO14 (5)
Fri 28–Sun 30   Gallagher English Premiership (5)
Greene King IPA Championship (5)
Sat 29   ARGENTINA v NEW ZEALAND
(TRC)
SOUTH AFRICA v AUSTRALIA
(TRC & MCP)
English National Leagues
Tennent's Scottish Premiership (5)
Tennent's Scottish National
Leagues
Welsh Principality Premiership (5)
Welsh National Championship

Sat 29/Sun 30   Tyrrells English Women's
Premier 15s

OCTOBER 2018

Fri 5–Sun 7   Gallagher English Premiership (6)
Greene King IPA Championship (6)
Fri 5/Sat 6   Guinness PRO14 (6)
Sat 6   SOUTH AFRICA v NEW ZEALAND
(FC & TRC)
ARGENTINA v AUSTRALIA (TRC)
English National Leagues
Tennent's Scottish Premiership (7)
Tennent's Scottish National League
All Ireland Irish Leagues
Welsh Principality Premiership (6)
Welsh National Championship
Welsh National Leagues

Fri 12–Sun 14   Greene King IPA Championship (7)
European Champions Cup (1)
European Challenge Cup (1)
Sat 13   English National Leagues
Tyrrells English Women's
Premier 15s
Tennent's Scottish Premiership (8)
Tennent's Scottish National
Leagues
Irish Leagues
Welsh Principality Premiership (7)
Welsh National Championship
Welsh National Leagues

Fri 19–Sun 21   Greene King IPA Championship (8)

Key: TRC = The Rugby Championship; BC = Bledisloe Cup; FC = Freedom Cup;
MCP = Mandela Challenge Plate; figures in brackets (14) etc. indicate the rounds of competitions.

	European Champions Cup (2)
	European Challenge Cup (2)
Fri 19/Sat 20	All Ireland Irish Leagues
	Tennent's Scottish Premiership
Sat 20	English National Leagues
	Tyrrells English Women's Premier 15s
	Tennent's Scottish National Leagues
	Welsh Principality Premiership (8)
	Welsh National Championship
	Welsh National Leagues
Fri 26–Sun 28	Premiership Rugby Cup (1)
	Greene King IPA Championship (9)
Fri 26/Sat 27	Ulster Bank Irish Leagues
	Guinness PRO14 (7)
	All Ireland Irish Leagues
Sat 27	NEW ZEALAND v AUSTRALIA (BC – Yokohama, Japan)
	English National Leagues
	Tennent's Scottish Premiership (9)
	Tennent's Scottish National Leagues
	Welsh Principality Premiership (9)
	Welsh National Championship
Sat 27/Sun 28	Tyrrells English Women's Premier 15s

NOVEMBER 2018

Fri 2–Sun 4	Guinness PRO14 (8)
	Premiership Ruby Cup (2)
Sat 3	ENGLAND v SOUTH AFRICA
	WALES v SCOTLAND
	IRELAND v ITALY (in Chicago)
	JAPAN v NEW ZEALAND
	English National Leagues
	Tennent's Scottish Premiership (10)
	Tennent's Scottish National Leagues
	All Ireland Irish Leagues
Sat 3/Sun 4	Tyrrells English Women's Premier 15s
Fri 9	Welsh Principality Premiership (10)
Fri 9 –Sun 11	Premiership Rugby Cup (3)
Sat 10	ENGLAND v NEW ZEALAND
	WALES v AUSTRALIA
	SCOTLAND v FIJI
	IRELAND v ARGENTINA
	FRANCE v SOUTH AFRICA
	ITALY v GEORGIA
	RFU Championship Cup (1)
	Welsh National Championship
	Welsh National Leagues
Fri 16	Welsh Principality Premiership (11)
Fri 16/Sat 17	Tennent's Scottish Premiership (11)
Fri 16–Sun 18	Gallagher English Premiership (7)
Sat 17	ENGLAND v JAPAN
	WALES v TONGA
	SCOTLAND v SOUTH AFRICA
	IRELAND v NEW ZEALAND
	FRANCE v ARGENTINA
	ITALY v AUSTRALIA
	RFU Championship Cup (2)

	English National Leagues
	Tennent's Scottish Leagues
Fri 23	Welsh Principality Premiership (12)
Fri 23–Sun 25	Gallagher English Premiership (8)
	Guinness PRO14 (9)
Fri 23/Sat 24	All Ireland Irish Leagues
Sat 24	ENGLAND v AUSTRALIA
	SCOTLAND v ARGENTINA
	WALES v SOUTH AFRICA
	IRELAND v U.S.A.
	FRANCE v FIJI
	ITALY v NEW ZEALAND
	English National Leagues
	Tyrrells English Women's Premier 15s
	Welsh National Championships
	Welsh National Leagues
	RFU Championship Cup (3)
	Scottish Premier Cup (1)
	Scottish National League Cup (1)

DECEMBER 2018

Fri 30 Nov–Sun 2 Dec	Gallagher English Premiership (9)
Fri 30 Nov/ Sat 1 Dec	Guinness PRO14 (10)
	HSBC 7s World Series (Dubai)
Sat 1	BARBARIANS v ARGENTINA
	English National Leagues
	RFU Championship Cup (4)
	Tennent's Scottish Premiership (12)
	Tennent's Scottish National Leagues
	All Ireland Irish Leagues
	Welsh Principality Premiership (13)
	Welsh National Championship
	Welsh National Leagues
Sat 1/Sun 2	Tyrrells English Women's Premier 15s
Thurs. 6	Oxford U v Cambridge U Women 11:30; Men 15:00 (both at Twickenham)
Fri 7–Sun 9	European Champions Cup (3)
	European Challenge Cup (3)
Fri 7/Sat 8	All Ireland Irish Leagues
Sat 8–Sun 9	HSBC 7s World Series (Cape Town)
	Tyrrells English Women's Premier 15s
Sat 8	English National Leagues
	RFU Championship Cup (5)
	Tennent's Scottish Premiership (13)
	Tennent's Scottish National Leagues
	Welsh Principality Premiership (14)
	Welsh National Championship
	Welsh National Leagues
Fri 14–Sun 16	European Champions Cup (4)
	European Challenge Cup (4)
Sat 15	English National Leagues
	RFU Championship Cup(6)
	Tyrrells English Women's Premier 15s
	All Ireland Irish Leagues

	Tennent's Scottish Premiership (14)
	Tennent's Scottish National Leagues
	Welsh Principality Premiership (15)
	Welsh National Championship
	Welsh National Leagues
Fri 21–Sun 23	Gallagher English Premiership (10)
	Greene King IPA Championship (10)
Fri 21/Sat 22	Guinness PRO14 (11)
Sat 22	Welsh Principality Premiership (16)
	Welsh National Championship
	English National League 1
	Tyrrells English Women's Premier 15s
Fri 28–Sun 30	Gallagher English Premiership (11)
Sat 29	Welsh Principality Premiership (16)
	Welsh National Leagues
	(Rugby event at Twickenham TBC)

JANUARY 2019

Fri 4–Sun 6	Gallagher English Premiership (12)
Sat 5	Guinness PRO14 (13)
	English National Leagues
	Welsh National Leagues
Fri 11–Sun 13	Greene King IPA Championship (11)
	European Champions Cup (5)
	European Challenge Cup (5)
Sat 12	English National Leagues
	Tyrrells English Women's Premier 15s
	Tennent's Scottish Premiership (15)
	Tennent's Scottish National Leagues
	Welsh Principality Premiership (17)
	Welsh National Championship
	Welsh National Leagues
Fri 18–Sun 20	Greene King IPA Championship (12)
	European Champions Cup (6)
	European Challenge Cup (6)
Sat 19	Guinness PRO14 (13) (one match)
	English National Leagues
	All Ireland Irish Leagues
	Tyrrells English Women's Premier 15s
	Tennent's Scottish Premiership (16)
	Tennent's Scottish National Leagues
	Welsh Principality Premiership (18)
	Welsh National Leagues
	Welsh National Championship
Fri 25	Premiership Rugby Cup (4) (3 matches)
Fri 25–Sun 27	Greene King IPA Championship (13)
Sat 26	All Ireland Irish Leagues
	Welsh National Cup (2)
Fri 25/Sat 26	Guinness PRO14 (14)
Sat 26/Sun 27	HSBC 7s World Series (Hamilton)
	Tyrrells English Women's Premier 15s

Sat 26	English National Leagues
	Tennent's Scottish Premiership (17)
	Tennent's Scottish National Leagues
	Welsh National Leagues

FEBRUARY 2019

Fri 1	FRANCE v WALES (20.00)
Sat 2	SCOTLAND v ITALY (14.15)
	IRELAND v ENGLAND (16:45)
	Premiership Rugby Cup (4 – 3 matches)
	English National League 1
	RFU Championship Cup (QF)
	Welsh Principality Premiership (19)
	Welsh National Championship
	Welsh National Leagues
	Guinness PRO14 (15 – one match)
Sat 2/Sun3	HSBC 7s World Series (Sydney)
Fri 8	Welsh Principality Premiership (20)
Fri 8–Sun 10	Premiership Rugby Cup (SF)
	Greene King IPA Championship (14)
Sat 9	SCOTLAND v IRELAND (14:15)
	ITALY v WALES (16.45)
	English National Leagues
Sun 10	ENGLAND v FRANCE (15.00)
Fri 15–Sun 17	Gallagher English Premiership (13)
	Greene King IPA Championship (15)
Fri 15/Sat 16	Guinness PRO14 (15)
Sat 16	English National Leagues
	Welsh Principality Premiership (21)
	Welsh National Championship
	Welsh National Leagues
	All Ireland Irish Leagues
	Scottish Cup (QF)
	Scottish National League Cup (QF)
Fri 22/Sat 23	All Ireland Irish Leagues
Fri 22–Sun 24	Gallagher English Premiership (14)
	Guinness PRO14 (16)
Sat 23	FRANCE v SCOTLAND (14.15)
	WALES v ENGLAND(16:45)
	RFU Championship Cup (SF)
Sun 24	ITALY v IRELAND (15.00)

MARCH 2019

Fri 1–Sun 3	HSBC 7s World Series (Las Vegas)
	Gallagher English Premiership (15)
	Greene King IPA Championship (16)
	Guinness PRO14 (17)
Sat 2	English National Leagues
	All Ireland Irish Leagues
	Tennent's Scottish Premiership (18)
	Tennent's Scottish National Leagues
	Welsh Principality Premiership (22)
	Welsh National Championship
	Welsh National Leagues
Fri 8–Sun 10	Gallagher English Premiership (16)
	Greene King IPA Championship (17)

Sat 9	SCOTLAND v WALES (14.15)
	ENGLAND v ITALY (16:45)
	English National Leagues
	All Ireland Irish Leagues
	Welsh Principality Premiership (22)
Sat 9/Sun 10	HSBC 7s World Series (Vancouver)
Sun 10	IRELAND v FRANCE (15:00)
Sat 16	ITALY v FRANCE (12:30)
	WALES v IRELAND 14.45)
	ENGLAND v SCOTLAND (17.00)
	Tennent's Scottish National Leagues
Wed 20 or Thur 21	Natwest Schools Cup Finals
Fri 22–Sun 24	Greene King IPA Championship (18)
	Gallagher English Premiership (17)
Sat 23	Guinness PRO14 (18)
	English National Leagues
	Tyrrells English Women's Premier 15s
	Tennent's Scottish National Leagues
	All Ireland Irish Leagues
	Welsh Principality Premiership (23)
	Welsh National Championship
	Welsh National Leagues
Fri 29–Sun 31	European Champions Cup (QF)
	European Challenge Cup (QF)
	Greene King IPA Championship (19)
Sat 30	English National Leagues
	Tennent's Scottish National Leagues
	BT Scottish Cup (SF)
	Scottish National League Cup (SF)
	Scottish National Bowl (SF)
	Scottish National Shield (SF)
	Welsh Principality Premiership (24)
	Welsh National Championship
	Welsh National Leagues
	Tyrrells English Women's Premier 15s

APRIL 2019

Thur 4–Sat 6	All Ireland Irish Leagues
Fri 5–Sun 7	HSBC 7s World Series (Hong Kong)
	Gallagher English Premiership (18) (including Sat 6, Bath v Bristol 'The Clash' at Twickenham)
	Guinness PRO14 (19)
	English National Leagues
	Welsh Principality Premiership (25)
Wed 10 or Fri 12	Students Finals day (Twickenham)
	British Universities & Colleges Finals
	Men's Final
	Women's Final
	AASE Final
Fri 12–Sun 14	Gallagher English Premiership (19)
	Greene King IPA Championship (20)
Sat 13	Guinness PRO14 (20)
	English National Leagues

	Tyrrells English Women's Premier 15s (SF) (TBC)
	Welsh Principality Premiership (26)
	All Ireland Irish Leagues
Sat 13/Sun 14	HSBC 7s World Series (Singapore)
Fri 19–Sun 21	European Champions Cup (SF)
	European Challenge Cup (SF)
	Greene King IPA Championship (21)
Sat 20	Welsh Principality Premiership (27)
	Scottish National League Cup (F)
Fri 26–Sun 28	Gallagher English Premiership (20)
	Greene King IPA Championship (22)
Sat 27	Guinness PRO14 (21)
	English National Leagues
	Tyrrells English Women's Premier 15s (F) (TBC)
	Scottish Cup Final
	Scottish National Bowl (F)
	Scottish National Shield (F)

MAY 2019

Fri 3–Sun 5	Gallagher English Premiership (21)
	Guinness PRO14 (QF)
Sat 4	Welsh Principality Premiership (28)
	English County Champs. (1)
	RFU Championship Cup (F)
	English National League 1 & 2 Play-off
	English National Leagues Divisional Cup Final
	Army v Navy (Babcock Trophy)
	Combined Services U-23 v Oxbridge U U-23 (both at Twickenham)
	National U 20s Final
Sun 5	RFU Junior Vase Final
	RFU Senior Vase Final
	RFU Intermediate Cup Final
Fri 10	European Challenge Cup Final (St James' Park, Newcastle)
Sat 11	European Champions Cup Final (St James' Park, Newcastle)
	English County Championship (2)
Fri 17–Sun 19	Guinness PRO14 (SF)
Sat 18	Gallagher English Premiership (22)
Fri 24/Sat 25	Gallagher English Premiership (SF)
Sat 25	GUINNESS PRO14 (F)
	English County Championship (3)
Sat 25/Sun 26	HSBC 7s World Series (London)

JUNE 2019

Sat 1	Gallagher English Premiership (F)
Sun 2	ENGLAND v BARBARIANS
	English County Championship (Bill Beaumont Cup – Final)
	Gill Burns Division 1 Final
	Bill Beaumont Div. 2 Final

RUGBY WORLD CUP 2019

The first match in the tournament will be Japan v Russia on Fri 20 Sept in Yokohama.